THE ANALYZING SITUATION

Other titles in the Series

THE ANALYZING SITUATION

Jean-Luc Donnet

Translated by *Andrew Weller*

Psychoanalytic Ideas and Applications Series

Routledge
Taylor & Francis Group

LONDON AND NEW YORK

First published 2009 by Karnac Books Ltd.

Published 2018 by Routledge
2 Park Square, Milton Park, Abingdon, Oxon OX14 4RN
52 Vanderbilt Avenue, New York, NY 10017, USA

Routledge is an imprint of the Taylor & Francis Group, an informa business

Copyright © 2005 Presses Universitaires de France

English Translation Copyright © 2009 International Psychoanalytical
Society

Originally Published in French as *La situation analysante*

British Library Cataloguing in Publication Data

A C.I.P. for this book is available from the British Library

ISBN-13 9781855757660 (pbk)

Typeset by Vikatan Publishing Solutions (P) Ltd., Chennai, India

CONTENTS

IPA Publications Committee

The International Psychoanalysis Library, published under the aegis of the International Psychoanalytical Association, is the product of the editorial policy of the IPA Publications Committee: to serve the interests of the membership and increase the awareness of the relevance of the discipline in related professional and academic circles, and to do so through a continuity of publications so that the benefits of psychoanalytic research can be shared across a wide audience.

The focus of the Library is on the scientific developments of today throughout the IPA, with an emphasis within the discipline on clinical, technical, and theoretical advances; empirical, conceptual, and historical research projects; the outcome of investigations conducted by IPA committees and working parties; selected material arising from conferences and meetings; and investigations at the interface with social and cultural expressions.

Special thanks are due to Salman Akhtar, who conceived this-project. He not only diligently brought together important but scattered papers on positive human attitudes and feelings, but also arranged outstanding colleagues from all around the world to write meaningful commentaries and updates on these neglected but important topics. We are indeed thankful to all these contributors for their dedicated work.

Leticia Glocer Fiorini
Series Editor

ABOUT THE AUTHOR

Jean Luc Donnet is a psychoanalyst in private practice in Paris, France. Between 1983 and 2000 he was vice director-practitioner, then director-practitioner of the psychoanalytical consultation and treatment centre of the Psychoanalytical Society of Paris (Centre Jean Favreau). His main works include; *L'enfant de ça* (with A. Green), *Le divan bien tempéré*, *Le surmoi Freudien et la règle fondamentale* and *La situation analysante*.

PART I

The adventure of the method

(I) The first chapter of this book, 'From the Fundamental Rule to the Analyzing Situation', was one of the three pre-published texts which were intended to introduce the debates at the 2001 IPA Congress in Nice on the theme of 'Psychoanalysis, Method and Applications'.

As I explained when presenting it to the Congress,[1] my initial limited project was to revisit the historico-structural turning-point which constitutes the articulation between the process initiated by the rule and the complex configuration of the analytic situation. It seemed to me that if I managed to identify sufficiently the methodological interest of this articulation, it might constitute a good starting-point for the discussions to come.

The manner in which the Congress unfolded made it very difficult for these discussions to take place. It showed, once again, that a real debate between analysts can only occur under favourable conditions; a comparison might be made here with the conditions of the frame and setting which make the transference process and its interpretation possible. It turns out that, in the psychoanalytic field, questions relating to the method also concern the modalities of inter-analytic exchanges whose concerns cannot be completely dissociated from those of intra-analytic exchanges.[2] Moreover, my text, which is very

3

caught up in, and coloured by, French psychoanalytic culture, was difficult to read for foreign colleagues unfamiliar with its way of approaching problems, especially as its imposed length had obliged me to write in an elliptical manner, an adventure which I refer to in 'The 'Sirens' Song' (Chapter 2). However, it was only retrospectively, after the Congress, that I fully realized what obstacles I had come up against. I had been led by the theme of the Congress to question not only the diverse meanings of the term *method*, but the particular difficulty of using it in the field of Psychoanalysis, the field of unconscious processes. This question has been present from the outset, and various answers have been given to it which are generally marked by the concern to link our discipline to the scientific method. But my personal interest did not concern so much the theory of the method as how the reference—whether explicit or not—to the method functioned between the analyst and the patient in the first place, and then between analysts themselves. Now it appeared to me that the use of this reference was often marked by conflicts which not only concerned the eventual divergences relative to the contents of the prescriptions but, more fundamentally, the very status and role of the method. In the course of my long experience of inter-analytic exchanges—I am intentionally leaving aside psychoanalytic literature—I have been able to observe how frequently our discourses *about* the method have been torn between those discourses which, starting from a position of control, quite naturally have their place within a theory of the technique, and those which, emphasizing the necessary freedom of the analytic couple and the analyst's subjective involvement, tend to become discourses *against* the method, with the latter being readily likened to a set of *applicable* prescriptions. A patent example of this kind of alternative can be observed, for example, in the positions held with respect to the frame of the analytic situation. Whereas, over the last thirty years, a genuine work of elaboration has shown the complexity of its epistemological status, its theorization, and the processual effects of its variations, discussions about it still often lapse into a regressive alternative between, on the one hand, respect that is too dogmatic, and, on the other, rejection that is too relativistic. This same type of split can be found with regard to the practical value of announcing the fundamental rule, considered by some as a sacred obligation and by others as anti-analytic. (Donnet, 1995a) I noticed that such a logic of splitting—which I am schematizing excessively here—existed in myself, since I had always felt it was equally necessary to affirm a certain control *and* to criticize the lure, the illusion, to which it left one exposed. The phenomenon seems to translate a sort of ambivalence towards the place the method has in the analyst's mind; otherwise it bears witness to the precariousness and, at the very least, the oscillating, fluctuating character of its position. It will be seen that my answer to this question is to be found in the specific status of the theoretico-practical gap in Psychoanalysis.

There was another point which particularly concerned me. We know that Freud expressed his preference for a historical account of his discoveries, including the development of his method, rather than for a synchronic, dogmatic exposition, and we also know that training institutes have generally manifested a contrary preference. Now it seems to me that the analytic method only really becomes intelligible from acquiring knowledge, and even more, from traversing its historico-processual vicissitudes. This is true at the level of the History (with a capital letter) of psychoanalysis. An eloquent illustration would be the destiny of the fundamental rule: emerging as foundational to the method, it underlies the possibility of discovering the transference "as such", that is, as a symptom; but this discovery was to lead to its own disqualification as an applicable guideline, assuring a stable function of the third.[3] And yet, is there any analyst who does not carry within him (or her) the principle of free association, inscribed within an obviously complex methodological context? What is valid for the History of psychoanalysis is just as valid for each analysand discovering and exploring the analytic situation: the utilization of the means of the method is inseparable from the diachronic organization of his experience of the transference. Lastly, during the course of the analyst's professional life, since his own analysis, the changes resulting from his clinical experience and his process of theorizing are accompanied by often profound modifications of his relation to his/the method. I am merely pointing out the tension, which, in the field of psychoanalysis, necessarily marks the oscillation between the pole of objectivity and the pole in which subjectivity inevitably comes into play. It seems to me that the writing of my text for the Nice Congress was burdened by a requirement, which remained implicit, to "present" structurally certain key points of the method and, simultaneously, to emphasize the radically processual dimension of their functional pertinence. I wanted to try and grasp the key aspects of the method as they are actualized in the analyst's mind during the session, as they emerge in response to the requirement for an eventual positive functionality of the countertransference.

(II) This problematic is obviously present in the major authors of psychoanalysis, starting with Freud, and one never grows tired of admiring the way in which he takes up *methodologically* the question of the ambiguity of the transference. It would be interesting to note in his work, but also in the work of Ferenczi, Bion, Lacan, Winnicott, etc., the traces of ambivalence with regard to the psychoanalytic status of the method, and to link them up with the context of their work. In Winnicott's work, in any case, it finds a crucial expression with the dialectical opposition between a *game* and *play*, between a game with rules and play without rules.

The discourse on the method depends on secondary processes, and claims allegiance to the Ego or to the Superego-Ideal. If the encounter with the *Unc.* inevitably calls the Ego into question, if it does not bring about a state of crisis, the reference to the method between the patient and the analyst inevitably undergoes a similar fate and appears, to say the least, defensive. The discourse of the method is thus inhabited by the paradox which makes it anticipate—if not prescribe—its own *fading*. In my Congress paper, I stress the opposition between positive prescriptions and negative prescriptions, whose purpose is to preserve the ingenuousness of the experience; but this opposition culminates in the negativization of any reference to the method. The work of the negative (Green, 1999) concerns the modes of actualization of the method in the course of analytic action. The tension between the conventionalization that is implied by any explicit reference to the method and the authenticity of the lived experience constitutes an essential aspect of the unfolding of the process; its variations are complex, but identifiable. The question is one of knowing what relations are formed between the presence/absence of the method, and the variations of the function of the third. The explicit or implicit character of the methodological reference is always significant during the analytic process:

— a transference interpretation, especially when it is *successful,* has an *additional* effect which is to re-signify implicitly the interpretive function of the method in a dynamic way which produces thirdness;

- a reminder of the fundamental rule or of the frame—a re-framing—constitutes an explicit superego reference to the method, which does not exclude implicit interpretive effects.

These key issues are already present in embryo in the matrix sequence free association–interpretive *après coup*. Of course, the implementation of shared associative thinking implies a set of conditions to support it, but these never efface, however, the random, uncertain dimension of the operation of *après-coup*.[4] This gap shows that the discovery of meaning is linked to the risk taken of losing it.

(III) As I was in the process of writing my paper for the Congress, I realised more clearly to what extent this *intrinsic* problematic of the method had marked my earlier questionings. It appeared to me, for instance, that the ambiguous status of the method corresponded precisely to the function that it occupied in the theoretico-practical gap as I had tried to describe it in my article 'Sur l'écart théorico-pratique'(Donnet, 1985), that is, a mediating function between the theory of the psychic apparatus and the practice whose very possibility it underlies. While assuring the necessary link between them, the method must also guarantee their sufficient disjunction in order to avoid the risk of a theoretico-practical collusion which would turn the analytic treatment into an application of established knowledge. The rejection of the method, mentioned above, may be interpreted as a radical way of guaranteeing the gap.

This elucidation, retrospectively, sustained my wish to pursue the distinction between analytic site and analyzing situation that I had proposed in 1995, in the introduction to *Le Divan bien tempéré* (Donnet, 1995b). I have since tried to explore this opposition further, particularly during the inter-analytic exchanges in which I have participated, whether they culminated in a publication or not. These confrontations allowed me to evaluate both its pertinence and its limits.

In my mind, this couple replaced the opposition between frame and process whose inadequacy proved obvious once, beyond the concreteness and intangibility which constituted the primary methodological value of the frame, its *transferization*, and the imaginary/ symbolic valencies which make it actively *enter* the dynamics of the process had been taken into account, as was the case, moreover, for the fundamental rule. The notion of 'site' was intended to recognize the already established dimension of psychoanalysis, the inaugural *introduction* of the means of the method. But it refused the rigidity of the frame, the temptation to confer on it a univocal causal function, or a value of identity for the institution. It put the emphasis more widely, but more ambiguously, on the integration of the frame within the coherent configuration which constitutes the functional logic of the ensemble *put at the patient's disposal.*[5]

During the inter-analytic exchanges, I found that those colleagues who made use of the notion of site, immediately and spontaneously attributed it with a diachronic dimension, speaking for example of the construction of the site.[6] I was persuaded that they were right, and that it was almost impossible to refer to the site in any other way than by evoking the modalities of its *introduction*-exploration between the patient and the analyst in their first encounters. The construction of the site is reminiscent of *La construction de l'espace analytique* by Serge Viderman (1970). My first idea of a site corresponded to the mixture of geography (structure) and history in which it soon becomes impossible to know whether the resources which sustain the transferential dynamic were already there when it was established or whether they were produced by its very development. I regretted that the images once attached to the signifier site had been contaminated by its extensive utilization in the field of computing.

The term 'analyzing situation', on the other hand, has conserved an eloquent resonance; the present participle analyz*ing* signifies adequately the primacy of the dynamic point of view and recalls the point of departure which for me legitimized the notion: the reference to Winnicottian transitionality makes it possible to account for the paradoxical link between the transference dependence and the autonomy which underlies the veritable instinctual (drive) introjections of the Ego.

Initially, the analyzing situation seemed to concern the analytic process, in situation, in its optimal or ideal form of the development and resolution of the transference neurosis. I subsequently realized that the term could—and even should?—be used for any treatment claiming allegiance to psychoanalysis, that is, any treatment based on the postulate of a transferential dynamic of the encounter. In all cases, and whatever the setting proposed, an essential issue at stake remains the functional appropriation of the site by the patient for the optimal utilization of its resources. The satisfying processual outcome is that the working situation *becomes analyzing*.

(IV) In the treatments of patients who are 'on the limits' of the analytic situation, the notion of a site to be constructed can throw light, I think, on some of the required methodological inflections. The particularities of their processes and of the transfero/counter-transferential uncertainties render the ways in which the patient has encountered the site and been able to structure a 'situation analysis' (*analytique de situation*) all the more crucial.

It frequently happens that, in spite of the overall adequacy of the gamble of the indication, the patient is faced *traumatically* with the inadequacy of this or that element of it—for instance, the lying position, the analyst's silent reserve, etc. Interpretation, and any modification of the frame or setting, risks being premature. The analyst is led to initiate forms of exchange conducive to a sort of *preliminary working through*. Its aim is not to *familiarize* the patient with his/her resistances, but with the resources of the site. The encounter is not envisaged from the standpoint of what it repeats, but from the angle of what it offers that is *new*. The analyst avoids the risk of putting himself in a position of manifesting knowledge about the patient but, by *recognizing what is happening*, he shows he has knowledge of the site. It is striking to observe to what extent these forms of exchange bring to mind the Winnicottian squiggle, a squiggle which is centred on the utilization of the means, on their *arrangement*. Moreover, the most eloquent descriptions of this rather vague field of preliminary working through are those that René Roussillon (1995) has proposed for the processes inspired by the *typical games* of Winnicott, concerning the development of primary symbolization. Further on, I will discuss what, since *Playing and Reality* (Winnicott, 1971), has made playing a precious model for the analytic method.

The preoccupation with this initial 'fit', with this appropriation of the means, is all the more important in that the risks involved in the interpretive process have proved to be very great when the analytic process has implied, ever increasingly, *deeper exploration* of the transference. The repetition which underlies these manifestations is connected with an ever more distant past, with object relations that are ever more *primitive*, and concerns in the last resort the very foundations of the constitution of the Ego and of the object, of the subject and of the other. To the issue of subjectivization is added that of 'subjectalization' (Raymond Cahn, 2002). The return of/to the past takes place in heterogeneous ways (representations, actings, etc). The transition from the repressed, potentially recallable history to the pre-history, which can only be constructed, marks a true hiatus. The dynamic of the transference can less readily be inscribed within a different context. The precarious nature of the diachronized organization of the transferential regression also stems from the discontinuities specific to the psychic functioning of patients. The intensity of the counter-processual or anti-processual movements (Bokanowski, 2004) confers an opacity on resistances such that their transferential meaning assumes a value that is sometimes approximative. The specific stakes of the transference on to speech are included in the more primitive stakes of psychic, and even somatic survival.

This processual complexity is a burden on the analyst's function. His free-floating listening must be exercised in different registers, successive or simultaneous; of course, his countertransference, as he knows, will be intensely solicited; he will have to trust in his belief in the possibility to put to the service of his function those aspects of it which are accessible to him. It must be stressed that the descriptions by the *pioneering* analysts of extreme forms of transfero-countertransferential actualization contributed to enlarging the ordinary basis of this function. The temptation arises to postulate that the countertransference can be put in the service of the analytic function: faced with the most regressive transference, it seems to constitute the ultimate recourse of the function of the third. But does not such recourse imply omnipotence? The reference to the countertransference can become a *symptom* of the method, expressing both the longing for omnipotence and the requirement to control it.

By itself, the deeper exploration of the transference affects the interpretive function. Up to a certain point, the principle holds good according to which, whatever form the transference takes, the *exactness* of the interpretation remains the decisive factor for the progress of the process; there must be a correspondence between the archaic nature of the transference and the archaic nature of the content of the interpretation, its adequacy in relation to the level of the anxiety and the conflict concerned. But the processual characteristics mentioned above mean that the decisions to interpret occur within a less precise context; they more necessarily imply the personal equation of the analyst and his/the theory. The depth of the regression and the intensity of the dependence mean that the interpretations acquire ever increasing weight, placing a proportionate burden on the countertransference. The form of the interpretation becomes a crucial issue when one is faced with the gap between the regressive experience and the linguistic utterance.

The return towards what is primal tends to efface the historicizing subject in favour of a genetico-structural perspective centred on psychic functioning. It would be tempting to say that the more the *postulated* transferential relationship is like a primitive relationship, the less it differs from the relationship to the analyst in person,[7] so that, at the heart of the experience of the transference, the perception of the gap between subject and function in the analyst is threatened. Ultimately, as Jean-Claude Rolland (2006) notes, the difference between the analytic relationship and the transference *as such* becomes infinitesimal. The adjective clearly indicates to what extent the difference is sometimes only sustained by the methodological postulate of the psychoanalyst. The general line of interpretation is generally obliged, in the absence of a possible interplay between the here and now, and the then and elsewhere, to confine itself within the transference relationship or rather in the relationship *here and now*. One can see that there is a risk of the analyst being led to reincarnate the object, the primordial other, in such a way that, his speech, which, for the patient, emanates from this all-powerful Other, becomes indistinguishable from a 'primal Speech' providing meaning; thus an alienating register of primary identifications is thereby reinforced.

The adventure of the method might sometimes, at the height of the transference regression, lead the analyst to *adopt once again something* of the position of the hypnotist. It is worth asking oneself if there would be a point of virtual reversal here relative to the initial *per via di levare* of the method, which we know very well is consubstantial with the analyst's ethics.

The Freudian method arose from the rejection of the hypnotic influence, which Freud nonetheless designated as the unsurpassable model of the power exerted by one mind over another. The method found its first justification in the refusal to exercise this power for the purposes of analyzing what underlies it, i.e., the unconscious transference. Its fecund postulate was to use the interpretability of the transference to *resolve* it sufficiently, opening the way to an authentic process of autonomization.

Clinical reality very quickly showed that force and meaning were mingled, that a transference was necessary *to* interpret the transference *to be* interpreted. When Freud came to conceive that psychoanalysis implied the turning round of suggestion against suggestion, he recognized that interpretation only exerts its effects within a relationship of complex forces.

It is not surprising that the deeper exploration of the transference, the search for its origin, generate, with the help of the countertransference, the risk of an interpretive *excess*, an *immoderateness* in which the conjunction of the meaning of the interpretation and the force of suggestion would be accomplished.

But the critical evaluation of the interpretive function also forms part of the history of the method. It has even sometimes led to the contrary excess of abandoning interpretation.

In fact, a large part of psychoanalytic research has been devoted to everything that occurs upstream of the symbolic register of interpretation, giving the impression that it should precede it, prepare it, and complete it. The development of studies relative to construction, to the containing function, to transformation, to representability, to primary symbolization, etc., show the interest taken in the emergence itself of psychic representation in its dialectical relationship with the diverse forms of the work of the negative (Green, 1999).

Thus in these ways the method proves itself capable of making the *analytic*[8] transference possible, and the question of suggestion continues to pose itself at the very heart of interpretation. Is the analyst not in a position to substitute himself for primary objects in order to make up for a deficiency which the increasingly decisive importance attributed to the object, or the reference to the primacy of the other, makes obvious?[9] Is there not a temptation here to see the analyst as implanting a sort of psychic prosthesis? This temptation is noticeable, for example, in the practice that has now become commonplace of referring to alpha function as a psychical graft from the psyche of the other, whether mother or analyst.[10]

This idea—like interpretive excess—evinces, it seems to me, the temptation to see the analyst as the *primum movens*, to escape the dimension of the *undecidable* that deeply characterizes the logic of the *encounter*, of the relationship in the field of analysis. It signals the difficulty of accepting the limits that this logic imposes on the method.[11]

3. If there is an area of activity in which the logic of the encounter imposes itself naturally, *with its limits*, it is the area of play; and this is why, as I have already pointed out, the reference to play has constituted a model for the analytic method. This model is all the more important in that play illustrates the complexity of the relations linking the experience of it with the rules that organize it. I have also stressed that the opposition between *game* and *play* condenses the adventure of the method.

Play—like free association!—is free in the sense that it can neither be imposed nor inculcated; nor can it be directly transmitted or learnt. From the ontogenetic point of view, it appears with primal spontaneity and develops through the acted-played exchange with the object—and toys; it is practised alone, by oneself—like in the wooden reel game—and if it is internalized as fantasy, it is always available for inscription and staging under suitable circumstances in reality.

In a bold formulation, Winnicott (1971, p. 41) says that the natural thing is playing, and that 'the highly sophisticated twentieth century phenomenon is psychoanalysis.'

By qualifying it as sophisticated, Winnicott is not afraid of stressing the *artificial*, highly regulated character of play; but this is because, simultaneously, he endows play with a fundamental value in the very structuring of the human psyche. Play is correlative with a transitional space which renews the Freudian conception of the duality of the pleasure principle/reality principle. By inscribing psychoanalysis within the history of culture, Winnicott shows that he is deeply faithful to the Freudian idea of a *work of culture*.

Since its origin, the linguistic history of the term 'play'[12] shows that its semantic field has always oscillated between the idea of free amusement—a metapsychologically evocative term!—and that of a set of rules which organize the play and define in advance the stakes involved. The opposition between *game* and *play* overlaps with the dialectical antagonism involved in the definition of play.

When Winnicott places the accent on *playing*, it seems to me that it is primarily to protest against a notion of play that is *too* regulated, which runs the risk, by becoming conventionalized, of giving rise to an analytic *false-self*. He is thinking perhaps of the interpretive compulsion of a certain Kleinism postulating the permanent equivalence between psychic process and unconscious fantasy. When he celebrates the *absurd* dimension of *playing*, Winnicott is affirming the potentiality of an unintegrated experience of the self, capable of linking itself up again with primary creativity.[13]

But the value placed on playing does not imply in any way the rejection of game rules: would it not be absurd to suppose that so-called regulated play proceeded from the mere application of rules? Indeed, the reception and the appropriate accompaniment of regression require of the analyst an opposition that is subtly regulated and regulating, notably with regard to his countertransferential participation.

With a neurotic patient, the presentation of the method is confined to making explicit the convention of the frame which is applicable, and of the fundamental rule which is a *game* rule. It is clear that it is by playing that one learns to play or, more precisely, that one discovers the *raison d être*, the intelligence of the rules, in such a way that a part of the playing—the exploration of the site—consists in exploring the subjectivizing gap between playing and the rules.

For a borderline patient, this gap often contains a danger of disorganization, which in turn arouses a search for ritualized, even fetishized rules. The activity of the analyst in the preliminary process of working-through consists in detecting the slightest indication of a sharable area of play, an outline of thirdness. René Roussillon shows clearly in the process of typical games the requirement that each act of play be followed by an implicit agreement as to the rules of the game. Far, then, from going in the direction of a virtual antagonism between the game and its rules, the analyst strives to minimalize the gap between them by switching back and forth between both poles.

For every game, the experience of playing surpasses the rules which necessarily organize it, goes beyond the explicit issues at stake which define success or failure, and transcends the eventually traumatic necessities which determine it. The gratuitousness which qualifies play designates its purpose of pleasure, but recognizes above all the powerlessness of its over-determination to explain it. Play is underpinned by its rules and its stakes, but they can, as we say, kill the game, paralyze the player(s) to the point of impeding him/them to *play the game*, a game which, to be played, involves taking risks and making mistakes. The temporalization of its random factuality, which requires agreed commitment, gives it its enigmatic enjoyment.

Winnicott (1968) emphasizes quite rightly that instinctual excitement spoils or threatens playing, and infers that playing is non-instinctual. Certainly, not all playing involves, as is frequently the case, phallic affirmation, or a certain degree of hypomanic euphoria. But should its enjoyment not be linked to the random but—'from the beginning'—very necessary instinctual transformation which we call sublimation?[14] The most mysterious thing about playing, when it is transforming, is the way that pleasure, which is its first aim, functions as a bonus of seduction, as bait which permits it to bolster the appropriation of rules, that is to say, ultimately, the appropriation of the symbolic constraint which structures it.

In his article 'Le jeu et le potentiel', René Roussillon (2004), tries to summarize this process, pointing out that playing starts out from an illusory freedom—the sense of its gratuitousness—and results randomly in an authentic freedom that is won over by symbolization through repetition. Between these two freedoms there will be a subjectivized internalization of the symbolic constraints.

By postulating that the complex problematic of the psychoanalytic method could ultimately be reduced to that of a method of play, 'the play of the interpreted transference', I do not think I have lost sight of what for me, constitutes the pertinence of the notion of analyzing situation and the importance conferred on the construction of the site.

The analyst's understanding of the rules of the game constitutes, for the patient, whoever he is, the basis of a 'function producing thirdness' which is often challenged by the vicissitudes of the transference. This is why the analyst must remain faithful to the logic of analytic play (Parsons, 1999), even in those moments when he is confronted with the patient's suffering most intensely and needs to share his affects most.

It is true that this fidelity can represent an impossible task—a task that is sometimes almost crazy. It has to be underpinned by a masochism that functions as a 'guardian of psychic life' (Benno Rosenberg, 1991). But the analyst's position does not exclude manifestations—humour for example[15]—through which he resubjectivizes his function.

Michael Parsons identifies a function of 'guardian of play in psychoanalysis', and I find this formula valid, especially if, as he points out, it includes the analyst's participation in the development of play. This function does not coincide with that of guardian of the setting, which evokes more clearly the idea of a referee whose job is to make sure that the explicit rules agreed upon by both partners are respected.[16]

The function of guardian of play is more internal, more essential. Like the function of guardian of the setting, it nonetheless shows that the analyst's relation to his/the method, during the session, implies a certain Superego-Ideal register. It is easy to see that transgressions of the setting, in spite of their meaningful value, frequently induce in its guardian a resexualization of this relation, which makes acting out of the countertransference more likely and is detrimental to the re-emergence of thirdness.

This is why it is crucial that the Superego-Ideal register is centred on the function of the guardian of play, of the spirit of analytic play. If there has to be something sacred in the analytic encounter, is it not the rules of the game?

Notes

1. See Chapter 2 'The Sirens' Song'.
2. See Chapter 3 'Clinical case reports, inter-analytic exchanges'.
3. See Chapter 1.
4. Author's note: The term *après-coup* is the French translation for the German term *Nachträglichkeit* , translated by Strachey as "differed action", which does not render the Freudian meaning. Since it was taken up by Lacan, the notion of *après-coup* has been explored at length in France with particular emphasis being placed on the 'resignification' which occurs between its two phases. By stressing discontinuity, the virtual symbolizing transformation stands in contrast to a genetic and developmental perspective.
5. See Part 2: 'For a Logic of the Site'.
6. See, for instance, M.-F. Dispaux, 'Aux sources de l'interprétation'. In 'L'agir et les processus de transformations', a paper read to the Congress for French-Speaking Psychoanalysts, *Revue française de psychanalyse*, 66, 5, 2002.
7. The schematic picture that I am outlining here is reminiscent of the opposition identified by René Roussillon between psychoanalysis of contents and psychoanalysis of processes.
8. It would be tempting to subsume this under the Freudian term of *transferability*, used in *Totem and Taboo*, in the sense of a capacity for displacement triggered by the taboo of contact extended to

the psychic, whose movement of contagion seems correlative to a progressive attenuation of the omnipotence of thought. The displacement seems then to be a condition of analogical similitude.

9. When Winnicott speaks of the necessity of repeating primary environmental deficiency, it is to emphasize the possibility of perceiving, recognizing, and elaborating it. The only correction that he envisages—inherent to the work of speaking during the session—is the correction of an eventual earlier denial. But it is easy to see how frequently the approach to early traumas slips into the idea of reparation whereby an infantile experience that was lacking finds its accomplishment in the analytic situation, without the question of *après-coup* (*Nachträglichkeit*) being raised.

10. Bion took care to present alpha function as a purely theoretical inference—like the masochistic phase in the second stage of Freud's analysis of the fantasy *A Child is Being Beaten*. The transformation of beta elements into alpha elements is situated, in the last instance, in the opacity of the intrapsychic, which makes it possible to suspend the genetic question of the distinction between the eventual roles of the mother and the analyst. It describes the transformations of projective identification through the containing function—including maternal reverie.

11. It thus proves impossible to define precisely, and even more so, to objectify what would constitute a specifically psychoanalytic per *via di porre*, complementary to the *per via di levare*. It is not that, in the reality of clinical practice, the treatment does not give rise structurally to certain suggestions—in the form of superego introjects—but it is not acceptable to integrate them within the deep logic of the method. Moreover, it would be interesting to compare the principle of *per via di levare* and contemporary research into morphogenesis which shows the mechanisms of a sort of structure of life (Ameisen, 1999).

12. *Jocus* means 'playing with words'; in French the term *jeu* comes etymologically from *joueur* (player): playing with words.

13. Playing concerns a psychic register far removed from that which is concerned by the *intentional* suspension of the conscious purposive idea, which, in the neurotic, provides the opportunity for a repressed idea or image to manifest itself. This gap gives an idea of the distance that separates the Winnicottian approach to play from that which had decisive importance in the discovery of the interpretation of dreams and which led Freud immediately to make a study of jokes, etc. One could say that this was the unconscious of the *first topography*, well-structured by the relations of the primary processes with the organization of language. This unconscious lends itself to interpretation which depends on a double meaning of words.

For a rigorous exploration of this register of play from Freud to Lacan, see S. Wainrib, 'Là où çà joue', *Revue française de Psychanalyse*, 68, I, 2004. The fact nonetheless remains that a link between these registers of play can be made in terms of the way that the symbolic constraint which is common to them is internalized. It would be worthwhile, in this respect, to read the whole of the volume devoted to play. I shall not return here to how the use of play by child psychoanalysts—and also psychodrama—has contributed to our thinking about play in adult psychoanalysis.

In one sense, Winnicottian playing challenges the unconscious determinism from which Freud started out. Lacan was to link this issue with the plays of linguistic signifiers. But, by replacing the repressed unconscious with the unorganized impulses of the Id, was not Freud himself opening up a path to a conception of the primordial psyche as deterministic chaos?

14. See J.-L. Baldacci 'Dès le début…la sublimation ?', paper given to the Congress of French-Speaking Psychoanalysts, 2005, in *Revue française de Psychanalyse*, 2005/5, pp. 1405–1474. See E. Sechaud, 'Perdre, sublimer', paper read to the Congress of French-Speaking Psychoanalysts, 2005, in *Revue française de Psychanalyse* , 2005/ 5. See the chapter in this book, 'Work of Culture and Superego'.

15. I would like to point out that, in this clinical context, recourse to humour can be pertinent, whereas an interpretation that is too close to a joke would arouse a sense of futility. (See J.-L. Donnet, 1997).

16. These rules would be less necessary if analytic play only consisted of the communication of already constituted fantasies. The integration of *Agieren* (acting out) implies that the "theatre of the I" (Joyce McDougall, *Théâtre du Je*, Gallimard, 1982) on the analytic stage coincides with certain characteristics of the *materialised* playing of the child and its risks of getting out of control. The structural significance of the *incident of the frame* stems from the fact that it corresponds to a potentially symbolizing breach of the site.

References

Ameisen, J.C. (1999). *La sculpture du vivant: le suicide cellulaire ou la mort vivant*. Paris : Seuil.

Bokanowski, T. (2004). 'Souffrance, destructivité, processus'. Report to the 64th Congress of French-speaking psychoanalysts in Milan, 2004. In *Revue française de psychanalyse*, 68(5).

Cahn, R. (2002). *La fin du divan*. Paris: Odile Jacob.

Green, A. (1999). *The Work of the Negative*, trans. A. Weller. London: Free Association Books. [Originally published as *Le travail du negatif*, Paris: Editions de Minuit, 1993].

Donnet, J-L. (1985). 'Sur l'écart théorico-pratique', *Revue française de Psychanalyse*, 49(5): 1289–1306.

Donnet, J-L. (1995a).'Le Surmoi et la règle fondamentale. Monographie de la *Revue française de psychanalyse*. Presses Universitaires de France,

Donnet, J-L. (1995b). *Le Divan bien tempéré*. [The well-tempered couch] Paris: Presses Universitaires de France, 'Le Fil rouge'.

Donnet, J-L. (1997). 'L'humoriste et sa croyance'. In *Revue française de psychanalyse*, 61(3): 897–917.

Parsons, M. (1999). 'The Logic of Play in Psychoanalysis'. *Int. J. Psychoanal.*, 80: 871–884.

Rolland, JC. (2006). *Avant d être celui qui parle*. Paris : Gallimard.

Rosenberg, B. (1991). *Masochisme mortifère et masochisme gardien de vie*. Paris : Presses Universitaires de France.

Roussillon, R. (2004). 'Le jeu et le potentiel'. In *Revue française de Psychanalyse*, 68(1): 79–94.

Viderman, S. (1970). *La construction de l'espace analytique*. Paris: Denoël.

Roussillon, R. (1995). 'La métapsychologie des processus et la transitionnalité'. Report to the 55th Congress of French-speaking psychoanalysts in 1995. In *Revue française de psychanalyse, 59*, Special Congress Issue, pp. 1351–1519.

Winnicott, D. (1968). 'Playing: Its theoretical status in the clinical situation' 1968, *Int J Psychoanal., 49*.

Winnicott, D. (1971). *Playing and Reality*. London: Tavistock.

CHAPTER ONE

From the fundamental rule to the analyzing situation

For André Green

"Though this be madness, yet there is method in't"

Hamlet, Act II, 211

I. Some key aspects of the method

(A) Any attempt to define the analytic method is immediately faced with the contrast between what the term method suggests in the way of controlled organization, and the renunciation of control implied by free association. No doubt this paradox of *methodic unreason* was necessary if the *Ucs.* was to open itself to rational investigation.

In its immanence, the method cannot be distinguished from the manner in which the psyche proves capable of producing an associative sequence and of discerning an unconscious logic in it afterwards. When one thinks about it, the method cannot easily be separated from the theory of the psyche which makes it possible to interpret the sequence and think about the hypothesis of the *Ucs.* In this respect, by writing *The Interpretation of Dreams* (1900), Freud went to the very heart of the matter: the telling of dreams and their interpretation finds its continuation in the theorization on the work which produces them.

(B) At another level, the method provides the link between this Freudian invention, its scientific reference (positivist) and the demands of clinical practice, which, as an applicable medical technique, needed to demonstrate its validity. Thus in accordance with the project of analysis cure, the method consists in carefully creating the conditions in which free association proves to be practicable, interpretable and beneficial. A contradiction emerges at the heart of these conditions between those based on acquired knowledge, theoretical and practical, and those which prescribe the suspension of this knowledge so that the encounter with the *Ucs.* is authentic. Knowledge does tend to predetermine the finality of the experience, and even to give the method a quasi-programmatic dimension. Hence the importance of the capacity to function *negatively* in order to preserve the loss of the ordinary references of meaning which the shared associative process entails, and also the hazardous dimension of the *après coup* in which there is an attempt to find meaning through interpretation. In addition to free-floating attention, a learned ignorance (Lacan) or negative capacity (Bion) are also qualities said to characterize the analyst in his work. This contradiction reveals the need for the element of thirdness, for which the method is the safeguard.

(C) Retrospectively, certain initial aspects of the method now appear to have been more or less adequate responses to this requirement, which became all the more imperative in that analysis needed to shake off the hypnotic 'influence'.

1. Freud's preference for a method operating *per via di levare* corresponded in part to his assertion that the analyst and the situation should introduce nothing foreign into the patient's mind. This asepsis meant that the method simply allowed unconscious processes to manifest themselves, and that interpretation merely revealed the meaning of what was already there in the repressed. Nowadays, no one doubts that the analyst and the analytic situation participate, *nolens volens*, in the structuring of the phenomena in process.
2. In the first place, the method postulates a conscious ego-subject, capable of observing a part of his internal world in order to make

it an object of investigation. The very development of the method would show how this ego is subverted by the *Ucs.* and how precarious the observer–observed distinction is (for the analyst as well).

It was difficult to get beyond theses initial responses which were often institutionalised. Evidence of this may be found, for instance, in Freud's attachment to the material truth of memories, before he was able to authenticate the conviction arising from a construction, and its indirect associative confirmation, and then sift out the notion of historical truth. Conceived of as a neutral agency of objectivization, the method seemed, in effect, to guarantee the objective validity of the knowledge acquired and the results obtained. Is it not the case that there is still a widespread conviction that the truth of analysis can be validated by studies aimed at objectivizing the initial development?

Psychoanalysis is currently exploring what it can learn from other scientific models (self-organisation, determinist chaos, new conceptions of history, etc.) which are compatible with the specific requirements of its own discipline.

(D) The function of the third party can no longer provide any sort of prior guarantee. Its specific role is one of *producing thirdness* (A. Green), an essential factor in the dynamics of a process which sometimes causes it to disappear.

The adventure of transference situates the desire for alienation, inherent in the intersubjective relationship, at the heart of analytic activity. There is always a risk that the experience will comply with the analyst's desire and his theoretical pre-conceptions. Freud draws attention to the unavoidable ambiguity of this when he says that, at a certain level, a hypothesis can no longer be distinguished from the phenomenon it relates to. This is why it is necessary to confer a specific value on the *gap between theory and practice* in analysis; for it is not *de facto*, but involves an ethical prescription which is related to the respect for otherness.

This gap is the object of a constant conflict in inter-analytic exchanges between the 'scientific' desire to fill it and the humanistic requirement to confirm its irreducibility.

(E) Due to the increasing complexity of the psychoanalyst's function, descriptions of method tend to be focused on his functioning, the modalities of which are sustained by his particular gifts, his own analysis and training, and ultimately inform his interpretative creations.

This description is rendered all the more accessible and open to theoretical elaboration in that the analyst combines within himself both subjective experience and his/the theorization. But for this very reason, it activates the self-referential danger which threatens psychoanalysis and the temptation to turn the psychoanalyst into an omnipotent 'technical subjectivity'.

1. This is illustrated, for instance, by modern theories of counter-transference. Originally, counter-transference was conceived of as something disturbing the analyst's function: this was a narrow point of view, but one which drew attention to the gap between subject and function, the symbolic support of the function. A wider theoretical outlook takes into account the structural character of the psychoanalyst's subjective involvement, as well as the principle of the potential functioning of that part of it which is accessible to him. This unquestionably results in broadening the basis of the function. But there is an increased danger of the gap between subject and function disappearing; either because, for example, the analyst ends up candidly making a function out of his subjectivity; or because he thinks of his function as being indefinitely relevant and malleable, once the counter-transference capacities are there. Yet, is it not necessary for the method to place an elaborative reference point (dialectical) between the limits of the analyst and the limits of the analysis—which after all are the correlate of its consistency.

2. Moreover, faced with a commonplace impasse in the transference–countertransference situation, the analyst quickly sees that the Ucs. remains the Ucs., and that his capacity to use his countertransference and self-analysis is strictly limited. What can he learn, then, from the method? Quite, simply, that it is necessary to go back to the beginning by doing another period of analysis or supervision. In so doing, he rediscovers the original challenge, i.e., speaking by associating in order to give a chance to the interpretative *après-coup*.

The listening situation, then, is part and parcel of the method: it is an inter-analytic annex of the analytic situation in which counter-transference can take the place of transference.

(F) Centreing the method on the analyst goes hand in hand with the temptation of merely seeing the patient as his beneficiary in order to describe the effects he or she has on him. One of the motive forces of my work has been to draw attention to the fact that the first meaning of the rule—making the patient the active agent of the method—survives the vicissitudes of transference; and, that it is the analysand, primarily, who makes the analyst an analyst. My experience as an analyst and consultant has made me particularly sensitive to the attachment that patients—even the most difficult ones—show towards the analytic situation with regard to *its specificity*, the logic of its functioning and its ethics; a sense of attachment which is distinct from—and sometimes in conflict with—that which they show towards the analyst. For them, it is a question of playing by the rules of the game, a key element in the function of creating thirdness. Something essential in the method is at play in the process of self-appropriation through which the patient becomes an analysand.

II. From the procedure to the rule

(A) It will be worthwhile to return to the definition Freud (1922, p. 233) gave of psychoanalysis in his Encyclopaedia article. He both linked and distinguished:

- the procedure 'for the investigation of mental processes which are almost inaccessible in any other way';
- and the method '(based upon that investigation) for the treatment of neurotic disorders'.

The transition from investigation to treatment corresponds to the shift from procedure to method:

- the procedure of free association can be used for pure investigation;
- the method lays down the procedure, which has become the fundamental rule in the 'structured' situation, resulting in a process of *transforming* investigation. This is why the method can be used *for* a treatment: the psychoanalytic cure consists of *additional* indirect effects, of psychical transformations inherent in the process. Notwithstanding the complexity that has been introduced, we still find the founding postulate of a truth which heals.

(B) Freud replaced the panoramic memory of the hypnotised subject with free association. It was up to the patient to actively suspend the exercise of his reason in order to grasp and communicate his incidental *unwelcome* thoughts. The procedure was only introduced originally to investigate an enigmatic phenomenon which was already there, i.e., that of symptoms and dreams whose meaning needed elucidating. There was a clear distinction, then, between this *fixed* object and the subject who participates, with the analyst, in investigating it.

This limitation of the procedure reflected that of the *Ucs.* conceived of as a lacuna.

(C) In spite of the simplicity of its formulation, the rule contained all the ambiguities which would lead to the analytic situation and its complexity.

1. By suggesting to the patient that he should say everything that comes into his mind, even if it seems nonsensical, unimportant or disagreeable, the rule combines the positive proposition to speak spontaneously, i.e., 'freely', and the *negative* prescription not to shut out incidental thoughts. It makes the *already existing* object of investigation disappear, which implies conventionalizing the spatio-temporal limits of the session; and, it suspends the implicit difference between those moments when the patient is speaking in his own name and others when he is talking nonsense while associating. However, it does not prevent the patient from bringing, at the beginning of the session, an object of investigation (an account of a dream, for instance) to which he will have some associations.

2. At the same time, however, announcing the rule favours psychical and discursive factuality in the *here and now*; it places the session under the *virtual* aegis of free association. The analyst, for his part, finds himself immediately in a position to listen associatively to the process of the session; there is thus a gap between the two protagonists which is part of the structural dissymmetry of their positions. The crucial question, with regard to the method, is to know how this dissymmetry can lead to a division of labour which is functional and not hierarchical since this gap involves a risk of alienation. Is there any analyst who has not been troubled by the observation that he has just heard a transparent associative process during a session in which the patient seems not to have wondered if he was saying something different from what he had intended to say.

3. This danger is inherent in the fact that the rule stipulates implicitly that the object of investigation will be produced in or as a result of the session. The patient's activity becomes, then, both the actual vehicle and the specific object of the investigation. How can the method ensure that concomitance exists between the production and the investigation of an object? Stated in this way, the question elicits but mediocre answers.

The first would be that of alternation. With the psychoanalyst's tacit agreement, the patient rediscovers the initial logic of the procedure: associative investigation follows the presentation of an object.

The second, a caricature, would be that of a permanent split, as in the metaphor of a train journey during which a traveller sitting next to the window describes to the person next to him the changing views he sees outside. The patient ensures there is a disjunction, without interference, between the associative production of a psychical film and a purely informative account collaborating with the investigation.

The third solution would be that of a permanent division of labour, the principle of which is that the analyst's listening *applies the rule* to the patient's functioning. Is it not the case that Freud expected the rule, in an objectivizing mode and in the third person, to provide an impartial guarantee that the forces involved in the conflict could be fully manifested? For the experienced analyst the rule is an analyzer of the whole of the patient's psychical functioning. From this point of view, it is the psychoanalyst's interpretation which constitutes, retroactively, the object of investigation, as a result of the choice of 'material' made in the session.

It can be seen that the division of labour makes the patient the producer, and the analyst the investigator. The patient is assumed to be subject to an internal split between subject and object (of investigation); since, in the final analysis, the interpretation has to be addressed to a part of his ego which has remained an observer.

4. The weakness of these responses shows that the rule introduces a rupture with the principle of objectivizing the procedure. The distinction between an immobilized object of investigation and its investigation by a conscious subject is erased when confronted with the intra- and inter-subjective logic of an investigation which transforms what it encounters and is itself transformed by the encounter. The process involves the subject's indefinite

experience of being decentred. The rule supposes that, through the heterogeneity of the signifiers employed (A. Green) and the diversity of the forms of enunciation, associative activity is no longer only a means: informed by the subject's self-division, it provides the opportunity for a tangible and troubling perception of *the other scene*; the experience of this drifting takes only one direction: 'the goal is the journey'. As in La Fontaine's fable 'The Labourer and His Children', associative exploration can end up by substituting the value of working-through for the discovery of the hidden treasure—the *predetermined* finality of the initial procedure.

III. Transference

The primacy conferred by the rule on here-and-now factuality inevitably implied that the transference would become the object of investigation produced *in* the session. But it also contained the idea that, as it was produced *by* the session, its interpretation required a renewed conception of the analytic situation.

(A) Within a short space of time, Freud (1914, p. 154) stated first that the theme of transference should only be interpreted once it had become a resistance; and then, that it proved possible to give a new transference meaning to all the symptoms of the transference-neurosis.

From resistance to interpreting, transference thus became the medium of an interpretative function which was obliged to comply with it 'methodically'. But we may wonder whether this progress was not paid for by a slightly restrictive systematic dimension.

(B) In 'The Dynamics of Transference' (1912), Freud refers to the 'immense disadvantage in psychoanalysis as a method' when speaking of the fact that transference, generally speaking the strongest factor in success, can turn into the most powerful vehicle of resistance. I do not want to go back over the way in which he proved that this was only a matter of appearance, and showed how the obstacle is changed into a vehicle of success. But it is not difficult to detect the signs of unease that transference and the exigency of interpreting it constituted for the theory of analytic method as he had conceived of it. I would like to highlight two of these signs:

a. Having pointed out that the stoppage of associations is always linked to a transference-idea, and observed that as soon as the 'explanation' is given to the patient the stoppage is removed, Freud (1912, p. 101) writes that in case of failure 'the situation is changed from one in which the associations fail into one in which they are being kept back.'

b. At the end of the article, and in a manner which stands out from the rest of the text, he emphasizes that the highly regressive form taken by the transference actualization is due 'to the psychological situation in which the treatment places the patient' (p. 107); and, as if to justify its necessity, he concludes '... it is impossible to destroy anyone *in absentia* or *in effigie*' (p. 108). It is clear that resistance in the transference raises the issue of the violence of interpretation as well as that of countertransference: the cause and consequence of the turmoil affecting the method.

It is not very difficulty to demonstrate this turmoil. To illustrate the 'putting into action' of transference (*agieren*), Freud cites as an example the case of a man who became mute when the fundamental rule was announced, owing to the displacement onto the analyst of a conflict with parental authority. It can be seen, then, that the rule, which is supposed, *a priori*, to further the investigation of an intra-psychical conflict, loses its status as a tool and becomes its unconscious factor on the analytic stage. It has lost its referential value of thirdness.

But it has not lost its functional relevance, since the patient has produced an interpretable transference symptom.

Nonetheless, a problem arises with regard to its eventual interpretation, particularly in the absence of an adequate associative context. Is there not a danger of it manifesting the analyst-father's knowledge and power; and of it being perceived—like the formulation of the fundamental rule—as resulting from the position which he occupies in the transference?

Thus, not only does transference disqualify the rule's function as a third term, but it tends to unite the interpreter and the transference-object, and to turn resistance towards analysis into resistance towards the analyst. This is surely an immense disadvantage for the method.

The objectivizing distance was indispensable for transference to be understood as a symptomatic phenomenon. By the same logic, its interpretation was seen as containing the principle of its resolution. But if transference is turned against transference, it also means suggestion is turned against suggestion (Freud), in which the reference to thirdness tends to be lost in the dual relationship, and meaning gives way to force.

If transference lends itself so readily to resistance, is it not also because its interpretation is too closely tied up with the aim of lifting its resistance, and perhaps of denying the analyst's desire? Exaggerating slightly, Lacan said that there is no other resistance to analysis than that of the analyst himself. You will recall the metaphor Freud employed to illustrate the impossibility of allowing the patient the right of reserve or asylum. Resistance would make its home there just as criminals would take refuge in churches if there was a round-up which respected their sanctuary in such places. Is it not the case that the exigency of relating everything that happens to the transference contributes to making transference the favoured refuge of resistance, in response to the round-up approach of the method?

IV. The analytic situation

(A) The dialectics of transference and its interpretation constitutes a source of methodological malaise owing to the ambiguity it introduces into the conception of the analytic situation. It was noticeable in a certain outlook which prevailed at the time of my training, which claimed that the situation was as neutral as the analyst and his mirror-function. It was supposed to guarantee the spontaneity of transference, itself a condition of its analyzability. However, this notion of spontaneity has long been marked by a striking ambiguity; for it has been understood as meaning that the analyst and the situation 'play no part' in the development of transference (instead of simply pointing out that the reserve of the former and the invariance of the latter make it easier to understand). Thus, in 1950, I. McAlpine caused a sensation by describing transference as *induced*, rediscovering what Freud had written in 1912. This occultation may be interpreted as an after-effect of the mourning of *neurotica*, and no doubt the requirement that no seducer should be subject to incriminations (for the psychical reality of the transference fantasy to be *objectivizable*) had its part to play.

In correlation with this, because the method was preoccupied for the most part with the lifting of infantile amnesia and reconstructing the past, transference was inevitably considered from the angle of its purely repetitive dimension; accordingly, its interpretation was supposed to uncover the contents of its amnesic memory (A. Green). From this point of view, interpreting the transference necessarily implied an aspect of refutation, rectifying its illusion by means of the 'neutral' reality of the situation.

(B) Insofar as the actualisation of transference represents the vehicle of analytic action, a more open and complex conception—but also more ambiguous—of the analytic situation is both required and permitted. It raises in a different way the question of creating thirdness.

1. On the one hand, there is no reason to describe transference as pure repetition; it displaces, invests, introjects and projects in a (more or less) discriminating manner. It is psychical work which is symbolic or potentially symbolising. It introduces *difference into repetition*, which was even more evident for Freud when, *à contrario*, he encountered transferences in which reproductions emerged of an 'unwished-for exactitude' (1920, p. 18), evoking a compulsion to repeat going beyond the pleasure principle.

   The spontaneity of transference can be seen in the way it erupts, takes advantage of circumstances and *creates a happening*. I am tempted to generalise Freud's metaphor on transference-love: a cry of fire is raised during a theatrical performance; for a while, one does not know whether it is part of the performance or whether the theatre is going to catch fire. Once one has decided not to call in the fire-brigade, the problem is how to let the performance continue while modifying it so as to be able to integrate the event afterwards. The precious ambiguity of transference is to give tension, more or less intensely, to the continuity of the plot and the discontinuity of the event. For Freud, the analytic situation falls half-way between fiction and reality; one should add between the 'here-and-now' and the 'then-and-elsewhere'. With his concept of the transitional area, Winnicott showed why it was essential that transference not be faced with the dilemma of being a real or a false fire: what matters is the spirit of play in which the ethics of transference is sometimes difficult to distinguish from the principle of the method.

2. On the other hand, the analytic situation is not 'neutral', in the sense of a pure projective surface. It is active in two ways: negatively, because it repudiates through the constraints it imposes; and, positively, because it contains something gratifying

and appealing too. Behind the necessary reserve of the manifest offer lurks a latent mixture of frustration and gratification: by proposing his two successive active techniques, Ferenczi simply accentuated what already existed.

The analyst and the situation are both *involved* in the structuring of the transference process: the principle of a permanent demarcation between the observer and observed is untenable. Moreover, there is scarcely any sense in claiming to be able to describe in an objective manner a direct causal effect of the instruments of analysis: the same element (the couch, the analyst's silence) can, depending on the patient and the moment in question, assume different, even contrary meanings.

(C) The process is thus the result of an *encounter* which cannot be reduced to determining factors: an encounter between the demand—the suffering—of the patient, and the analyst in question. But, in the last resort, it is an encounter *between two differences: that which sustains the transference and that which distinguishes the analytic situation from any other life-situation.*

The dynamics of the transference stem from the potential of the encounter: they are nourished by what the situation has to offer to transference investments, quite apart from the analyst's contribution as a person; the investigation by the patient of his internal world can scarcely be separated from the use he makes—for the most part in silence—of the resources of the *site*[1]. One can thus speak of a *situation analysis*[2] (as one speaks of a situation comedy) linked to the mobilisation of a *compulsion to represent* (J.C. Rolland) which is simply sustained and accompanied by stating the rule.

This compulsion occurs at all levels of psychical *représentance*,[3] from that which is nearest to the psychical delegation of id impulses, or alpha function (Bion) to that which depends on the systems (ego–super-ego) connected with language. It is remarkable that already in *The Interpretation of Dreams*, Freud had described an antagonistic equilibrium in the session between the narcissistic regressive tendency of figurative thought processes, attracted by hallucinatory fulfilment, and the anti-regressive tendency of objectalizing speech. He did not separate, therefore, the '*psychization*'[4] of the drive and the socialization of the psyche, repudiating in advance the false dilemma between drive and object.

On the contrary, the acting-out of transference marks speech with the stamp of hysterical acting. Its major concern is to introduce a portion of the hallucinatory charge of unconscious phantasy into speech. It is this factor which gives the analytic situation and interpretation their specific economic and dynamic dimension.

An enactment which is so charged with affective potential presupposes that all the means provided by the situation are used; that is, figurative regression, which makes the session an equivalent of the system sleep-dreams, makes use of the site, the couch and the environment, even if only in order to negativise them perceptively. Speech implies addressing the invisible other and, in so doing, makes a demand on him (Lacan), which means transference. But the enunciation invaded by acting and affect implies a transference *on to speech*; a temporary transformation of the psychical apparatus into a language apparatus (A. Green).

'Situation analysis' realises the singular, variable configuration of these various forms of transference; and, the question of knowing whether and how transference onto the analyst may be distinguished from transference onto the analytic situation is crucial for the method and the function of thirdness.

(D) If I am insisting on situation analysis, it is because the particular use the patient makes of the resources occurs relatively independently of the analyst's interventions, enabling him, in a sufficiently autonomous manner, to become an *analysand*.

We know how far attempts to teach the patient his task as an analysand, to explain how to use analysis, are more or less vain. In order to account for an appropriation which constitutes a re-invention, it is necessary to refer to the *paradoxical nature of Winnicott's idea of 'found-created'* which basically corresponds to the creativity involved in the spontaneity of transference.

The analyst's role in this appropriation is, first and foremost, not to hinder it; but there are no guarantees. Although one of the most constant functions of his silent listening is to be found here, it has to be noted that an 'additional' effect of interpretative interventions is to show the patient that he is using the situation advisedly, even if negatively.

Here, I am doing no more than point out the extent of the methodological problem posed by including the interpretative function among the resources of the site; particularly where the transference interpretation uttered by the analyst is concerned.

The extent of the problem can be measured in terms of what separates, beyond their understandable differences, two extreme models:

- in the first model, which is very widespread in France, a sort of renunciation of interpreting has resulted in making the silence of the analyst's listening the essential aspect of his role;
- in the second, an intensive and systematic interpretative activity indicates a sort of *obligation* to interpret, the correlate of which is that the analyst then has to find in his theory the means to defend it.

By laying emphasis on the autonomy the patient has in making personal use of situation analysis, I certainly do not mean to justify the analyst's fetishistic silence. On the contrary, the patient's autonomy may enable the essential resource of interpretation to free itself from an obligation which meant that free association would only consent to give up control over meaning if it could be made up for later on.

In fact, interpretation, when it is mutative—whether it originates from the analysand or the analyst—comes *when it wants*: it is a matter of *après-coup*; and its emergence is uncertain and unpredictable. Even if it falls within the continuity of the process, it takes effect through the discontinuity of its emergence, of its metaphorical significance. Its additional effect, then, is to rediscover, to *produce* the disjunction between the analyst as interpreter and the analyst as transference-object. This effect of creating thirdness is jeopardised, and even annulled, when the transference does not introduce an element of symbolising difference into what is being repeated. One of the fundamental questions concerning the analytic method is to know whether interpretation can make transference analyzable, or if the situation must rely on pre-symbolic effects.

If interpretation is not to acquire the addictive value of providing meaning, it is necessary, as we have seen, for the patient to have been able to invest the couple activity-passivity specific to associative activity, even when the latter serves the work of remembering, (re-)constituting his own history and self-interpretation. The analysand does not attempt to apply the rule, but he reinvents it by giving meaning to the dimension of play it offers, the unknown outcome of which remains to be discovered. Perhaps he senses rather quickly that the implementation of the rule is an outcome of the process, and that its deepest implications are closely tied up with the principles of mental functioning which are the foundation of the theory of the analytic method.

V. The analyzing situation

As it is commonly used, the term 'analytic situation' quite rightly combines the analytic action and the space-time in which it unfolds.

I think it would be useful, nonetheless, to distinguish between the analytic *site* and the analyzing situation:

- the analytic site contains the ensemble of what the offer of an analysis constitutes. It includes the analyst at work.
- the analyzing situation results, haphazardly, from the sufficiently adequate encounter between the patient and the site. It implies the subjectivized use, through the experience of 'found-created', of the resources of the site and their singular configuration by the patient.

Why the analyz*ing* situation?

First, in order to stress the depth of the metapsychological issues involved in appropriating the site and the self-representations implied: for instance, the analyst's silence sustains the crucial experience of solitude in the object's presence. But this experience is not necessarily made explicit or interpreted. As with an iceberg, only a small part of the density and complexity of the process appears on the surface. Discourse on the method tends to ignore the silent process of working-through on the intra-psychic level. The notion of the analyzing situation is an attempt to get beyond—by integrating it—the dialectic 'transference neurosis–working alliance' in which the role played by the alliance appears to be too reasonable.

Secondly, to underline the specific functional unity constituted by the ensemble 'analysand-analyst-situation'. That is to say, a binding unity between the patient's intra-psychic processes and their externalization on the stage of transference; but also between the mental processes of the two protagonists, to the extent of realising, through the interplay of transference and countertransference, an activity of co-thought, a field (Baranger), a partial fusion, by bringing into play primitive identificatory processes, i.e., a shared area of play.

The analytic framework makes it possible to contain the complexity of these entangled processes; but the bilateral internalization of what it represents symbolically is what enables it to ensure, through its materiality, the vicariousness of the element of thirdness at the height of transference–counter-transference crises and the extreme situations they give rise to (R. Roussillon).

Through the self-regulated interplay of these exchanges, the analyzing situation takes the form of a structure integrating the analysand-analyst couple in its capacity for self-organization, as well as the dynamic processes of its disorganizations-reorganizations.

Thirdly, and finally, to indicate that this structure is the vehicle of a self-investigating dynamic, arising from the potential of the encounter. The process unfolding within the analyzing situation has its own trajectory and is informed by the immanence of a terminable analysis. Ultimately, this end can only be defined by *the exhaustion of the resources of the site*, as it has been actualised, at a given moment in the relationship between such and such a patient and his analyst. This temporality, which is included in the very dynamics of the transference experience of illusion-disillusion—which is so lacking in interminable analysis—ensures the latent presence of a function creating thirdness which is actualised through interpretation.

It sheds meaning on the paradoxical words of a patient at the heart of his transference process: 'I come to my session to ask myself why I come'. The process owes temporality its capacity to be 'the exploration through speech of the transference experience' (Rolland, 2006).

Addendum

In memory of S. VIDERMAN

To illustrate the way the rule works, here is a scene from the beginning of my own analysis, forty years ago: my memory of it has retained the intensity of a screen-memory.

1. It concerns a session which was to end at 8 p.m. Sensing or anticipating that it was about to end, I stopped talking. In the silence, the church tower nearby marked out eight strokes. The sign I was expecting was not forthcoming and instead my anxiety increased.

I exclaimed: 'But I don't want you to give me more than my time'. I was both surprised and reassured by what I had just said. My analyst then ended the session.

2. I would like to draw attention here to those aspects of my recollection which remain for me the most striking.

a. The *contrast*, first of all, between my conviction that I had used the situation in a way that was both new, improvised and in accordance with its potentialities, and, what for me, was the altogether enigmatic dimension of the scene. This contrast shows that the feeling of being an analysand is not necessarily linked to providing meaning through interpretation.

b. My conviction was based, on the spur of the moment, on the actualization of all the different elements of the site, i.e., the framework (the set time for ending the session); the setting (the scene is unthinkable without the couch and the immanence of the standing position); the analyst (the supposed guardian of the framework and object of the transference); and finally, the rule (I will come back to this).

This unexpected conjunction of circumstances gave me the feeling that I was the author of the whole scene, that I had created what was already there.

c. My conviction was also based on the memory-trace of the transformation which had occurred and been provoked by my enunciation: at the beginning, I was addressing my analyst through action; at the end, I felt that my enunciation had emerged from somewhere far off and had touched me closely, but it was enigmatic and not unpleasant; I can recall just how much the experience of this process needed the support of the analyst's silence.

3. Some comments retrospectively:

a. Later on in my analysis, as a result of interpretation and working-through, I was able to discover the various facets of the seduction fantasy of/by the adult which had been actualised on the stage of transference and expressed transparently under the cover of negation. It was no easier to integrate the traumatic resonance of the eight strokes of the clock, evoking the inexorability of time, separation and death.

It seemed to me, then, that in the scene, what I had said had had the effect, through my identification with the voice of the super-ego ideal, of making me the one who decided the moment of ending in order to avoid being subjected to it.

My pleasant feeling of being an analysand was perhaps above all an expression of my satisfaction at having taken the place of the one who was safeguarding the frame. Was this a maniac defence or an experience of 'found-created'?

In any case, the analysand's autonomy cannot be located—any more than the working alliance—outside the field of transference and its interpretation. It can, occasionally, be interpreted as a defence against the experience of dependency; but who would this interpretation be addressed to if this transference dependency was not given metaphorical form by the transference itself?

  b. In the scene itself I did not say (scrupulously) to my analyst, 'I am feeling anxious about the idea that ...', and even less 'I have just had the fantasy that ...'. My enunciation had the status of an acting-out. How, then, did this form of acting-out use the analytic situation more fully than the two others which would have been the expression of an insight?

First of all, it involved the experience of confusing, projectively, the analyst with the other—whoever it was who wanted to keep me—before I re-found the person of whom I would not have gone as far as to say that I 'had always known' that he was going to end the session; and that, by identifying with me, he was leaving me the time to say: nothing can replace the fact that 'returning to oneself comes about by making a détour through the other' (A. Green).

It was also the complexity of what was happening in the *gap* between psychical factuality (the affect of silence, hearing the clock, increasing anxiety) and speech:

– firstly, the anxiety was enigmatic and the enunciation ego-syntonic (I know what I do not want);
– secondly, my enunciation, which relieved my anxiety (repression), then became enigmatic and, in this sense, it was offered to the analyst by the analysand. It assumed the value of a *signifier*. It is the ensemble of this 'mix-up' which has an irreplaceable subjectivizing significance.

The underlying issue here is that of a privileged mode of overcoming the barrier of repression: from the point of view of interpretation, this is accomplished through the associative linking occurring between anxiety and the denied representation of a demand for love. But compared with a mere insight, acting-out involves an instinctual introjection; it transfers onto the act of speaking the hallucinatory power inherent in the unconscious wishful fantasy. *Speaking hysterically is an ersatz for hallucinatory satisfaction.*

The transference actualization underlies the possibility of conceiving the effect of interpretation as being similar to a *wave of symbolization*, containing an optimal conjunction of force and meaning.

Notes

1. The term 'site' might perhaps have been translated as 'setting'; however, for the author, particularly as a French speaker, the word 'site' has an echo with the term *'situation analytique'*; and, furthermore, his original use of it carries a signification which he feels is broader than the term setting. Cf. Donnet, J.-L. (1985) *Le Divan bien temperé.* Le fil rouge, P.U.F. [transl. note].
2. The French here is: *'analytique de situation'.* [transl. note]
3. A general category including different types of representation and which implies the activity, the movement of representation. [transl. note]
4. The process of rendering psychic. [transl. note].

References

Freud, S. (1900). *The Interpretation of Dreams. SE*, 4–5: 1–621.

Freud, S. (1912). *The Dynamics of Transference. SE*, 12: 99–108.

Freud, S. (1914). *Remembering, Repeating and Working-Through. SE*, 12: 147–156.

Freud, S. (1920). *Beyond the Pleasure Principle. SE*, 18: 1–64.

Freud, S. (1923 [1922]). *Two Encaeclopaedia Articles. SE*, 18: 235–259.

Rolland, JC. (2006). *Avant d'être celui qui parle.* Paris: Gallimard.

CHAPTER TWO

The Sirens' song

(I) In accepting to present one of the texts designed to open the discussions of the IPA Congress in 2001, my intention was to return to a subject that I had already explored, namely, the crucial articulation between the fundamental rule and the analytic situation. The fundamental rule is an extension of the original procedure for investigating the unconscious: free association. The analytic situation arose from more or less contingent conditions, but ones on which it came to confer the value of a structural ensemble that is necessary for initiating the project of analysis.

The text presented was concerned with this theme but, so I was told, it was so condensed and elliptical that it was difficult to read. It may even have seemed like an attempt to present the analytic method in a dogmatic, synthetic way.

Nothing was further from my intentions, which shows that writing—like analysis—is a largely unpredictable adventure. Initially, the only approach possible—in conformity, moreover, with a certain Freudian preference—seemed to me, on the contrary, to be one of historical exposition; it was a question of revisiting certain points that had constituted stumbling blocks, or points of emergence, in the history of my relations with the method, which, naturally, I supposed would find echoes in other analytic histories.

The trap of writing was that this process involved the evocation of three distinct, but profoundly interwoven chapters in my memory: Freud's inaugural invention; my discovery of the method in my own analysis; and the appropriation of the method transmitted during my years of training at the Paris Institute and at Jacques Lacan's Seminar. The writing of each of these chapters got off to a good start and the difficulties they presented seemed to find an echo as I passed from one to the other: I was on my way for 2001, *An Analytic Space Odyssey* ... In fact, I noticed that I was confirming the truth, concerning the exposition of the/my method, of what Freud had described in 1912 with regard to the conduct of the treatment: only the first moves are *calculable, methodologisable*. I very soon came up against the obstacle of the complexity at work in history, but also in a process of remembering, which made me aware of changes of perspective, of shifts that had occurred in my way of seeing things, without my realizing it. It is significant that the aspect of the method that remains the most well *introjected* is related to the transcendence of a belief, to the lifting of an internal resistance, to a sudden emergence. How could the history of our appropriation of the method be related linearly when, by definition, it is marked by our relation to the unconscious, to our transference on to analysis. We can appreciate the limits of the pertinence of certain didactic expositions of the method, whose programmatic value sometimes seems to imply that the analytic process itself can be described and conducted according to a linear developmental model. And yet, I do not think we should attempt to eliminate what necessarily belongs to the superego in the methodological reference, underpinning its subjectivizing appropriation. By virtue of the objectivity of its discourse as a third term, the method resists the temptation to regard the analyzed mind of the analyst as the alpha and the omega.

(II) My writing odyssey was suddenly interrupted by the need to produce a text whose length had to be severely limited. So I assembled a montage in which something of these three chapters subsists:

– I maintained, in the form of an addendum, which could also have been a prologue, one of the screen-memories of my own analysis. It illustrates the way that a signifying moment of the process is

combined with an introjection of the functional ensemble constituted by the analytic situation.

- Of the history of the Freudian discovery, I have essentially kept
the transition from the *procedure* of free association to the fundamental rule which constitutes, from a retrospective vantage
point, a truly epistemological rupture. The procedure utilizes free
association in a delimited, *conventionalized* way, in order to elu-
cidate an unconscious object that is *already there*; the rule seems
to extend its logic when it requires the patient to speak so that
he/she becomes an active partner in the work. But it will subvert the subject-object relation because the object has to be produced through the session, which will be the *transference*; nothing
conventionalizes more the distinction between the moment the
patient associates and the moment he speaks in *his own name*.
Since everything happens under the aegis of the rule, the door
is open to a reversal whereby the analyst's floating but informed
listening is in a position to hear everything that the patient says *as*
free association. The rule thus eventuates in a profound crisis of
the function of the third that it was supposed to provide, a crisis
that is contained by the frame, but to which symptomatic theorizations will attempt to respond—for example, the theory of the
autonomous ego allied to the analyst's reality-ego.

In fact, the truth of the rule is to create an analytic process wherein
the function of the third can emerge from the very investment of
the associative drift and from its stimulus through interpretation,
of whose success it is a token. The most pertinent notions such as
field, co-thinking, analytic couple, chimera, and the emphasis given
to the countertransference, are correlative of the effacement of a permanent third term which claims to remain extrinsic to the process.
Without aiming to do so, the fundamental rule has opened out on
to a transfero-countertransferential processual adventure in which
the frame itself is caught. It is not surprising that, for many analysts,
announcing the rule has become obsolete, and even anti-analytic.
The session nonetheless still remains under the aegis of its ethic; and
the mode of functioning that it seemed to require as a means proves,
in its approximate realization, to be a remarkable indication of the
transformations aimed at by the method. For those analysts, like
myself, who consider its enunciation to be appropriate, it has the

interest of signifying indirectly to the patient the analyst's mode of listening, and the implicit designation of a function producing third-ness still to be discovered.

Regarding the methodological issues of my years of training, I have retained a few points relating to the interpretation of the trans-ference. At the beginning of the 1960's, the reference to the Freudian *per via di levare*, to an analytic situation as neutral as the analyst's mirror function, was still part of a background indicating the contra-suggestive preoccupation of the method, and ensuring an optimal relation between the spontaneity and analyzability of the transference. At the same time, however, it was accepted that the analytic situation was active both due to its frustrating effects and its seduction. The transference was considered as a re-edition of object-relations, with-out contradicting the instinctual nature of its dynamics. There was a lively debate around its creative potential, its capacity for symboliz-ing or proto-symbolizing emergence, akin to the transference opera-tive in the dream-work.

In the middle of this somewhat confused vortex, I recall having been very struck by the critique that Lacan made of an interpretation of the transference, which, by emphasizing its anachronism, would reduce its illusion through the confrontation with the simple reality of the situation. Lacan's critique was addressed to *Ego Psychology*. Now, there was no representative of this theory in my group—and no one interpreted the transference in this way, except, of course, in the context of a counter-transferential movement. I was thus especially sensitive to the primacy of the symbolic register and of the function of speech that Lacan emphasized as a counterpoint to the duality of the orders of the Real and the Imaginary. I also retained a certain reticence with regard to systematic interpretation of the transference which risked conventionalizing the process. This is why Winnicott's concept of transitionality helped me to give clearer shape to the dia-lectical relation between the transference and its interpretation. It was important that the experience of the transference should not be confronted, through the interpretive formulation, with a dilemma which could concern the actual or the past, which could be spontane-ous or provoked, projective or well-founded. In a process which goes its own sweet way, interpretation does not need either to confirm or to refute the reality in the transference. Of course, this is an optimal position which is characteristic of the *analyzing* situation. And one could describe difficult analyses through the prism of what can give the transference access to a 'transitionalization', that is to say, to a primary symbolizing capacity. When reading Bion during the years 1965–1975, I did not fully realize that this was what alpha function was about. The ambiguity of the transference is to be preserved or to be produced; its dynamic, which governs the process, is thus the fruit of the encounter between *two differences*. It is certainly possible to objectify both terms of the encounter. On one side we have the transferential phenomenon identified by Freud as a symptom; and, on the other, the *analytic site* with its frame, its fundamental rule, and its analysed and trained analyst. But this objectification, which is useful at a certain level, comes up against a stumbling block when it is a question of accounting for the analytic process. By speaking of the encounter between two differences, I am trying to recognize the undecidable: in the repetition which defines it—which can go as far as pure repetition—the transference is *postulated* as the vehicle of a difference, a movement of investment which creates the event. As for the analytic situation, a *radical* difference distinguishes it from every past situation; and this difference allows it both to be and not to be a re-edition of the past—for example, of an early object-relationship. Its difference and its capacity of equivalence make its encounter with the transference propitious, as a virtual vehicle of a difference in its repetition. The transference can thus be considered as an interpretation of the analytic situation; the transference interpretation, an interpretation of this interpretation, is also transference. It is in this way that the dialectic of the transference *for* interpreting and of the transference *to be* interpreted unfolds.

(III) To conclude, I would like to come back to the paradoxical nature of the psychoanalytic method.

The Freudian point of departure was the discovery of *the fact that truth heals*. The method presents itself, in the first place, as the procedure to follow or use in order to arrive at this truth from the moment there is an unconscious. The purely interpretive approach evinces the structural relationship between the end and the means: for the analyst, the maxim '*qui veut les fins veut les moyens*' signifies that the consistency of the results stems from the rigorous nature of the means employed. The Freudian idea of 'cure as an additional benefit' thus confirms the necessary autonomy of the method.

As the method learns from experience and becomes more complex, while claiming to be faithful to the original postulate, it is necessarily deeply modified owing to the clinical knowledge that it has to integrate. The analyst is no longer only someone who, along with his patient, is searching for the truth; he is someone who knows that not all truth is worthy of being spoken, and who thinks he knows on what conditions interpretation is possible, receivable, efficacious and useful. The accumulation of knowledge may tempt the analyst to use this knowledge directly. A legitimate pragmatic concern tends to confer on the method a quasi-programmatic dimension. Now, in the field of interpsychic forces activated by the transference, the method, although it arose from the rejection of the hypnotic influence, is always in danger of privileging, and even of producing the phenomena which confirm its prediction, or its predilection. The risk is aggravated by the demon of doing therapeutic good and the obligation to achieve results. This is why, at the heart of the prescriptions of the method, a special place must be given to the negative conditions which remind the psychoanalyst of the importance of suspending knowledge in favour of the quest for truth. Basically, Bion's negative capacity and Lacan's learned ignorance are merely an extension of Freud's floating listening. The paradox of our method is thus to have to foresee, and even to prescribe the *fading*[1] of the control to which it aspires like any method. The authenticity of the encounter with the unconscious and the experience of the transference presuppose the risk involved, the uncertainty of the adventure, the sub-traumatic register of the event. Basically, the paradox of the method is comparable with that of any project of expedition involving risks. The sailor, the example, knows that only sound preparation and navigation, as well as very rigorous manoeuvres, can bring him the control, the mastery, necessary for the success of his odyssey; but he also knows that the value of the experience remains fundamentally linked to its adventurous dimension. One can observe, in these times of democratic tourism, specialized agencies proposing organized trips in which the guaranteed existence of risks vies with the cover against risks.

I recall that I once used the episode of the *Odyssey* in which Ulysses hears the Sirens' song to illustrate this dimension of the analytic adventure. In order to protect himself from their ruinous seduction and to conciliate the wish to preserve himself with the satisfaction

THE SIRENS' SONG   47

of his desire, Ulysses, as we know, had himself bound to the foot of his mast (prohibition of acting) by his crew whom he asked to seal their ears with wax—and how can one fail to note that the analyst's training, which is first and foremost aimed at opening his capacity to listen to the unconscious, also implies that he is more or less immunised against the traps of the transference. At what point did this technical arrangement have to be put into operation and when could it be lifted? To be able to make this decision, Ulysses and his crew needed to know in advance everything that could be known about the Sirens, and also the topographical navigational bearings which would indicate to them—by identifying seamarks—that the dangerous channel had been crossed.

It can be seen that Ulysses, according to the usual definition of the term method, had planned *a series of operations defined in advance with a specific goal in mind.* I have always wondered if, faced with this programmatic mastery, and contrary to what Homer recounts, the Sirens had not abandoned their song.

Note

1. In English in the original.

CHAPTER THREE

Clinical reports, interanalytic exchanges[1]

(I) I would like to say once again that the points I have identified and proposed for discussion, with a view to examining the problematic of the method in psychoanalysis, derive their eventual import from the historico-cultural moorings of the subjective implication they reveal. It is *only* from this historico-subjective dimension that a truly interanalytic confrontation can emerge. The babelism of our exchanges can certainly be discouraging; it becomes interesting if one considers it as a phenomenon illustrating the clinical material of interanalytic exchanges, material which has its own consistency, its symptoms, and whose processes reflect, in particular, the contradictions present in the explicit or implicit conceptions that we form of the method which *should* govern our exchanges. For example, one of my discussants expressed the conviction that our differences should be dealt with and resolved by a rational method, according to objective criteria. One cannot deny that this conviction was part of the scientific inspiration of the Freudian perspective. I pointed out to him, however, that the method he recommended was completely foreign to the one that inspires us during the sessions. Should we acknowledge that there is a radical hiatus between the intra-analytic

49

and inter-analytic exchanges? If not, should we not ask ourselves questions about the methodological principles which guarantee the analytic specificity of our exchanges?

(II) If I leave to one side for the moment the activity of theorization, I find that the link between the session and the interanalytic exchange is constituted by the case report: it serves as a medium for the confrontation of our experiences in a practice which ultimately remains private, intimate, not to say secret. It seems necessary that these reports should not only be considered as truthful, but heard in terms of their manifest content, and, ultimately, as if they could coincide with the facts that they narrate—could it be, for example, that they reflect counter-transferential movements? This perspective stems from the demand for objectifications; it sustains in the exchange the idea that a case exposition can justify or contest a point of technique or theory, and that progress can result from this. The function of case reporting at this level is to enrich common experience and acquired knowledge in such a way that the method is able to derive precise indications, and even *technical applications* from the process. To the extent that such a definition remains compatible with a certain empirical adaptation, it is true that, by virtue of the vision and points of reference that it provides, it has its place in interanalytic practice. Clinical knowledge contributes to the mastery of operations, including those aimed at helping the patient to discover the means that the situation puts at his/her disposal.

This perspective leads one to wonder about the capacities of the method to integrate these acquisitions concerning the reality of a cumulative progress. Some analysts go as far as to postulate that the *analytic game* is entirely calculable. But the very principles of the method, it seems to me, are radically opposed to such a perspective.

(III) Listening to a report as if it repeated *exactly* what took place should not make us lose sight of the fact that it is a *fiction*: the reporting is always *retrospective*—whether it concerns a whole treatment or just one session. Recapturing this dimension of fiction leads us to another important meaning of the term method—namely, *the possibility of reconstituting the path one has travelled along in order to reach an aim, even though one was not clearly aware of it*. It is immediately clear that this definition is particularly adequate for the analytic field, even at the level of the sequence free association-interpretive *après-coup*.

Its microprocess implies that the path followed is reconstituted retrospectively by the patient's associations without his realizing it. More broadly, the suspension of the conscious purposive idea presupposes an investment of the associative path, since it is the retrospective understanding of the purposive idea which will, *to some extent*, endow it with its necessity.

The definition of the method as retrospective is equally valid for the clinical report which is necessarily a reconstitution of what happened. This is why, even when it appears to be coincident with an action which in reality it *reedits*, its truth is to retrace the *path* of a *discovery* rather than to confirm—or invalidate—the validity of a pre-existent method.

A particularly clear illustration of this is the situation of supervision or secondary listening. We know how counterproductive it can be when an analyst who is giving an account of a treatment is purely concerned with exactitude and wishes to demonstrate his mastery of the method. The analytic value of his account arises from a partially unconscious memory, which attempts to re-establish the different staging points of the journey. The adventure is not devoid of risk—a risk which, basically, is inherent to any clinical case report: *producing the unconscious in the very act which evinces its relative integration*. Accepting the subjective dimension of the report makes it the origin of a *new event* that is comparable, up to a certain point, with that which occurs in the session. The secondary listening situation means that the counter-transference *speaks itself*—which is something quite different from speaking of one's counter-transference. Moreover, the counter-transference does not have to be interpreted for the reporting of a case to modify its process. Every analyst knows from experience that a change will occur in a case that he presents. Which is why the situation of supervision—and more generally the interanalytic exchange—is to be considered as subsidiary to the analytic situation, extending the method's function of producing thirdness. In the history of psychoanalysis, the counter-transference only emerged as a concept through the existence of sufficiently conflictual interanalytic exchanges.

To say that truthful clinical reporting produces the unconscious is to say that it opens itself up to interpretation, that it gives it fresh impetus. In our exchanges, it is easy to see the omnipresence of this impetus, even when conventions impose its restraint. I think this interpretive openness is structural insofar as interpretation knows no limit, any more than the production of the unconscious. Interpretation refuses the closure of reporting.

If the sole function of clinical reports was to enrich shared experience and to perfect the method, we would not be able to explain their huge redundancy. Does their repetition not translate the need to retrace indefinitely the path of a discovery because it remains *adventurous*? It is undeniable that the reports contribute to the predictive dimension of the method. But this contribution is limited. There remains a considerable gap between the hypercomplexity revealed by reconstitutions and the programmatic value of prescriptions.

(IV) I thus think it is useful—contrary to the point of view expressed by Otto Kernberg—to maintain a distinction between method and technique. Technique belongs unambiguously to a register of application which knows in advance what has to be done, and which has the advantage of being transmissible and pertinent from the point of view of clinical thinking which is interested in what is *typical*, i.e. the typical aspects of psychic functioning as well as the preferred modalities for treating them. The analytic method transcends this register to the same extent that it foresees and requires its transgression through the issues at stake in subjectivity. I would thus be quite tempted to reserve the term method for a restricted corpus of fundamental principles which are sufficiently generous and abstract to discourage the fantasy of a cumulative technical mastery—principles whose employment necessarily involves *interpretation* by the analyst and the patient. Basically, the fundamental rule condenses these principles which, at the same time, explain why it is not made for being applied but for being interpreted. I will just return to a few crucial points:

1. The processual postulate of a transferential dynamic of instinctual (drive) origin linked to the encounter and tending towards psychic and discursive representation.
2. The primacy of associative thinking (free association/evenly suspended listening), implying that the processual sequence of the phenomena (representations, actings, affects, personal body states, etc.,) prevail over the meaningful content of each of them.
3. The principle of a compromise between the requirement of a *sufficient* interpretive *après-coup* and that of an experience of the unconscious and *of its irreducibility*.

4. The principle of a transitionalization of the transference, on which the contribution of its interpretation to symbolizing elaboration depends.

(V) I have put forward the idea that the clinical report produces technique by manifesting its mastery of the unconscious, and produces the unconscious by showing, like the analysand's speech, that it says more than and something different from what it thinks it says. But it also produces theorization about which I will just say a few words. To the fiction, according to which the clinical report relates facts, corresponds the idea of a theory which accounts for the how and the why of these facts. This is reminiscent of a positive, if not positivist theoretico-practical dialectic. Clinical facts are sufficiently objectivized to confirm or invalidate a point of theory: Popper's principle of falsifiability is defendable. It is true that Freud and some others after him knew how to allow a clinical phenomenon to challenge their theory, which, from the standpoint of sound method, was treated as *scaffolding*. But the history of psychoanalysis scarcely illustrates such a relation between practice and theory. It is sufficient to note that the immense work accomplished was correlative to the theoretical pluralism we are familiar with. That said, this pluralism is not necessarily a sign of weakness if we consider, with reference to Quinn's theory, that in a complex epistemological field, incompatible theories can have comparable pertinence. But it discourages the temptation of a totalisation. Our theories differ in particular with regard to the conceptions they form of the relations between theory and practice. Moreover, the relations between the analyst and his/the theory are very varied. There are those who claim to be disciples of one master, with the effects of coherence and theoretical closure that that implies; and others, no doubt the large majority, who put together a theoretical *hotchpotch* whose references form a rather vague ensemble that is often split and thus scarcely susceptible of being contradicted by clinical work. Globally, it can be seen that analysts hold to their theory more than to reason: it is the object of belief, of belonging, sometimes almost fetishized.

Perhaps the fragmentation of theoretical references and the crisis concerning the status itself of theorization throw light on the renewed interest for the *question of the method*. In the same way as it connects and separates the patient and the analyst by its reference to a third term, the method joins and separates theory and practice by situating itself at their interface. These principles can only emanate from a theory of the unconscious mind and of its transformations; and they say in particular why and how it is necessary for theoretical knowledge to be suspended during clinical practice. The risk is equally present of a practice without theoretical support and of a collusion between theory and practice which would turn the treatment into a pure application of knowledge. The method thus serves as the guardian of the gap between theory and practice. If analysts continue indefinitely to tell each other stories of analysis, it is in an attempt to fill this gap, but more profoundly to confirm its irreducibility.

Note

1. Written version of the concluding oral intervention at the IPA Congress, 2001.

CHAPTER FOUR

For a logic of the site: On the difference between psychoanalysis and psychotherapy

I. Is analytic treatment psychotherapy?

The current situation leads us to revisit the muddled question of the relations between psychoanalysis and psychotherapy. A first difficulty stems from the fact that the opposition between the two terms, which has a long history, is centred on two related issues:

- on the one hand, it corresponds to the limit between what is or is not considered as psychoanalytic; and thus to the limit of the specific field of psychoanalytic practice;
- on the other, it evokes, within this field, the difference between the analytic treatment in the strict sense ("psychoanalysis") and what we have become accustomed to referring to as psychoanalytic psychotherapies.[1]

It is difficult to treat these two limits separately because the way we establish the difference between psychoanalysis and psychoanalytic psychotherapy depends, to a large extent, on how we delimit the field of psychoanalytic practice.

It is clear that psychoanalytic psychotherapy lies at the intersection of psychoanalysis and psychotherapy, in such a way that it both upholds and threatens the principle of a unity of analytic practice. My immediate conclusion from this is that it is necessary to think *simultaneously* about what constitutes the unity *and* what constitutes the diversity, and even the heterogeneity of this practice.

In a recent article, focused on the impressive clinical case of a patient followed once a week (and in an institution) in the face-to-face situation, Marilia Aisenstein (2001) argues convincingly in favour of a principle of unity; which is why she gives her article the provocative title 'Psychoanalytic psychotherapy does not exist'. Marilia Aisenstein certainly does not mean to say by that that the work accomplished did not have a therapeutic aim: quite the contrary. She simply contends that it does not differ in any essential way from what would happen in the analytic situation, even with patients who are less ill.

The provocative nature of her title thus raises a symmetrically provocative question: is psychoanalysis not a form of psychotherapy? Is it not true that the work in a standard working situation,[2] when it is correctly indicated and well conducted, constitutes the most reliable and the most consistent of the psychoanalytic therapies? Is this not what leads us to propose it as the option of choice when it seems adequate and realizable?

What, though, makes us say so naturally: 'psychoanalysis is not psychotherapy'? And one very often gets the feeling that the negation establishes a link between the affirmation of the identity of the first, and a certain pejorative attitude towards the second.

We can see here, as I pointed out above, the trace of a long history in which the questions about the origin, the theoretico-practical development of the psychoanalytic field, the conflictual diversity of its socio-cultural inscriptions, and their ideological colourings, are interwoven.

I will limit myself to a few remarks aimed at delimiting the (psycho)therapeutic sphere in psychoanalysis.

The two terms emerged almost simultaneously towards the end of the 19th century, as a continuation of moral treatment. Marcel Gaucher and Gladys Swain date the medico-scientific baptism of psychotherapy from 1893 (Bernheim, Dubois de Berne, Dejerine) and link it to the exemplary confrontation between suggestion and persuasion. For them, it was in the intervening period that Freud invented his method, which he was to 'patent' in 1904 by entitling one of his technical articles 'Freud's Psychoanalytic Procedure'. Psychoanalysis thus made its appearance as a specific form of psychotherapy.

From the outset, however, it was already something more and something different with the appearance of *The Interpretation of Dreams* (1900), as the *Three Essays* (1905b), *The Psychopathology of Everyday Life* (1901) and *Jokes and their Relation to the Unconscious* (1905a) would soon show. The theory of the *Ucs.*, manifested its general anthropological import by linking the normal and the pathological, the individual and the group, etc.

Owing to the interactions between practice and theory, psychoanalysis developed as a fundamental discipline of the mind.

Why did its link with this discipline mean that analytic treatment found itself excluded from its original field of psychotherapeutic practice?

A first answer to this question would be to regard this exclusion as a consequence of the autonomy that its very development conferred on psychoanalysis. At the beginning, Freud needed medical backing for his procedure. But, in 1926, ('The Question of Lay Analysis'), he pointed out that the conduct of analytic treatment owed little to medical knowledge, that it could be carried out by laymen, and that its practice required specific training. His essential preoccupation was to remove psychoanalysis from the danger of subservience to medicine, and history has clearly confirmed the reality of this risk.

It is probable that the very term of psychotherapy is a vehicle of this danger because it evokes the weight of medical power in the (general) field of therapeutics.[3] This would explain why the rejection of the term (and of the thing) go hand in hand for many analysts with a particularly restricted and reductive version of what therapy is. However, defending the autonomy of psychoanalysis and the specificity of its procedure or method does not imply the need to caricature the medical (notably psychiatric) act. Psychoanalysis and medicine have large zones of overlap (for example, psychosomatics) calling for convergent elaborations. I have not forgotten Lacan's witticism: 'Real medicine is psychoanalysis', nor the definition of health proposed by Canguilhem: 'The margin of tolerance for the 'infidelities of the milieu'. The question of results, of psychoanalytic cure, cannot be envisaged by restricting therapy to direct action on the symptom: it involves the confrontation with complex models (immunology, for example).

In Freud's work there is an interesting ambiguity, moreover, concerning the place of cure in psychoanalysis. In his definition of 1922, the method ('for the *treatment* of certain neurotic disorders') occupies a *central* position between the investigative procedure (free association) and 'a collection of psychological information obtained along those lines, which is gradually being accumulated into a new scientific discipline' (1923 [1922], p. 235).

A bit later, however, once the theoretical corpus had become more organized, it seemed sufficient for the purpose of defining psychoanalysis, which possessed a number of applications, among which *therapeutic applications*. These, obviously, concern the whole range extending from the gold of analysis to the brass of psychoanalytic psychotherapies.

A reversal of the relation to the theory would mark the change of status of the notion of cure in the field of psychoanalysis.

In 1922, the method of investigation was used *for* the treatment, underlining its *autonomy* with regard to therapeutic aims. It is based, via the procedure, on the investigation of processes *almost inaccessible in any other way*: it is thus the irreplaceable form of a transformative investigation in which theorization finds the truthful source of its elaborations. If we add to this the observation that, in the training analysis, the method is employed without any explicit therapeutic aim, we find ourselves faced with the ingredients which led—in France particularly—to opposing psychoanalysis radically to any form of psychotherapy.

The method is at the centre of its definition, and the process of the treatment, of any treatment, comes to represent psychoanalysis as a whole: it concerns itself metonymically with its deepest anthropological questions, and it is then described as an experience with subjective implications that are so radical that they seem incommensurable with those of psychotherapy.

From this perspective, which expresses an ideal of analysis, the indicator of idealisation would be the depreciation of the 'therapeutic', assimilated to a social norm foreign to the analytic spirit.

It is important to realize, though, what led Freud to designate the treatment as a 'therapeutic application'. The formula clearly translates

Freud's conviction that the truth of analytic theory was sufficiently established so that it no longer needed to depend on its therapeutic successes. Freud was confirming, to some extent, a discordance between theory and practice, which is not contradicted by the picture of a therapeutic method that masters the means by which it operates. To be sure, the term application is embarrassing, suggesting an erasure of the gap between theory and practice: practice could lose its power of challenging theory. The risk arises, then, *under the pressure of therapeutic aims,* of making direct use of acquired knowledge, conferring on the method a quasi-programmatic dimension.[4]

It is these internal contradictions to psychoanalysis which give all its importance to the idea of *cure as an additional benefit.*

The formula is Lacan's, but its meaning is made very explicit by Freud (1923, p 251): 'The removal of the symptoms of the illness is not specifically aimed at, but is achieved, as it were, as a *by-product* if the analysis is properly carried through'.

It is a question, then, of the necessary autonomy of the method which does not imply any disinterest for its therapeutic effects, but postulates rather that their substance will depend on the strictness with which it has been employed: to ensure cure is not just transference, the transference must be analyzed. If it is useful to remind ourselves that cure is a by-product, it is because there is a temptation for the analyst who is confronted with the patient's suffering to give up interpretation for the uncertain alternative of fine-sounding words, that is to say, suggestive magic: Michel Fain has designated it as the 'demon of doing good'.

The first meaning, which still has currency, was accentuated by the encounter with training analysis where it seems possible to be able to dodge the therapeutic question. Thus the idea emerged of *'analysis for the sake of analysis',* placing value on a process which has its own finality, separate from any extrinsic reference. One step further, and there emerged the theme of pure analysis,[5] freed of any therapeutic objective, which had now become an impurity. *Pure* psychoanalysis coincided—notably with Lacan—with the psychoanalysis that was qualified originally as didactic, whose impurity, symmetrically, was its teaching aim.[6]

Is not pure psychoanalysis thus doomed to the pure transmission of a self-referential truth to which the analysand might well make a gift of his mind for the purpose of confirming and enriching the theory?

It is not surprising that this line of thinking tends to cover the collusion between subjective experience and adhesion to a theoretical-group Superego.

The therapeutic dimension makes its return by the usual means of being caught up narcissistically in the shared Ideal, the support of a false identificatory cure or recovery: this has always constituted the most tenacious resistance in training analysis. The idea of pure psychoanalysis thus becomes specious when, by becoming confused with didactic aims, it suggests a pure investigation pertaining to science, an analytic project without clinical foundations, and thus removed from the *postulate of a beneficial effect*.

It is true that the analyzing situation, through the dynamics of its process, can evoke, if not pure psychoanalysis, at least analysis for the sake of analysis. As any form of purposive idea—whether it is didactic or therapeutic—is suspended, there is a patent disjunction between the employment of the method and the expected results. However, this disjunction is only functional if the underpinning of these results by the process is guaranteed by a metapsychological equation specific to the transference neurosis. But this underpinning is not guaranteed.

Before returning to the methodological implications of its precarious status, I would like to emphasize that the expected cure consists of indirect effects, at some distance from the psychic transformations inherent to the process. The ambiguity of these effects is that they do not only depend on the analysis; that they come into play and are inscribed in heterogeneous realities; and finally, that they escape, to a large extent and quite naturally, the analyst's perception.

As for the specific psychic transformations, they are linked to the method, to the delimitations that it gradually operates in the patient's world while privileging psychic reality, the experience of the transference, and the acts of speech.

Such, then, is the ambiguity of the notion of cure in analysis: it is analytic insofar as it involves transformations, but it cannot be reduced to that, as is indicated by its status of *by-product*.

To illustrate this ambiguity, I will recall how Freud (1937, p. 219), in *Analysis Terminable and Interminable*, considers the reasons—satisfactory ones—for which patient and analyst bring their meetings to an end: 'Two conditions must have been approximately fulfilled: first, that the patient shall no longer be suffering from his symptoms, and shall have overcome his anxieties and his inhibitions; and, secondly, that the analyst shall judge that so much repressed material has been made conscious, so much that was unintelligible has been explained, and so much internal resistance conquered that there is no need to fear a repetition of the pathological processes concerned.'

As can be seen, Freud brings into play a duality of points of view which extends the dissymmetry of the analytic situation. But the point of view lent to the patient is external: the patient feels freer (less inhibited), calmer (less anxious); he no longer suffers from his symptoms (whether they have disappeared or are less disturbing). The triad Inhibition—Symptom—Anxiety does not refer to the mere negation of disturbances, but to the positive health of an autonomous subject ('more capable of loving and working').

The analyst's point of view remains internal to the method: it is an objective evaluation of the process and transformations acquired (making the repressed conscious, giving meaning to the enigmatic, working-through of resistances, etc).

This retrospective evaluation allows him to count on a sort of immunization concerning the repetition of pathological processes: the positive health of an Ego capable of managing the 'infidelities of the milieu'.

This theme, which is taken up in the rest of the article and directly linked to the second topography, shows how Freud had entirely abandoned the idea of a complete analysis, whose term would be as natural as that of a pregnancy: it is in the asymptotic temporality of the *so es war* ... which is translated well by the repetition of the quantitative 'so much ...'.

There is no doubt something a bit forced in the division of the two points of view: for the analyst is concerned by his patient's life; and the patient, having become an analysand, does not separate the value of his recovery or cure (even partial) from the means by which it has been achieved and which include the relational experience of the transference.

The division made by Freud has the major interest of showing that recovery in psychoanalysis can only be evaluated in terms of the conjunction of specific transformations *and* of their effects in the patient's life. It would be tempting for analysts to confine themselves to the specific transformations appreciated through the intra-analytic prism: for there is a real risk of these effects becoming the object of objectivizing evaluations depending on extrinsic criteria directly subjected to re-existing norms; but the self-referential risk is just as great. Is it conceivable, for example, that an analyst might consider as successful a treatment whose process—albeit substantial—has nonetheless resulted in a disaster in the patient's life? I am not referring here to any obligation to achieve a result, any more than I am referring to the power to decide what would be good for the analysand. I am simply making the point that the project of cure postulates, in the last instance, that the employment of the method will lead to a beneficial effect. By virtue of the initial evaluation that the indication implies, the analyst vouches for the pertinence of the method, which includes this postulate—*whether it is already there or to be produced.*

The *by-product* character of psychoanalytic cure thus assumes a structural value: the functional autonomy of the method is inhabited both by the fact that its finality must not be determined, and by the virtual presence of its (psycho)therapeutic vocation.

The analytic project is part of a social practice, which, however private it may be, and in order that it may remain so, needs a certain recognition from the social institution. The expected results of the treatment need to find expression in a valorized referential discourse that can be shared with the socio-cultural third party: they cannot be incompatible with the ideals (plural) of the cultural Superego.

This is why the term of 'cure' or recovery, which Nathalie Zaltzmann (2000) has explored in depth, is appropriate on account of its very polysemy. The verb 'cure' is transitive and intransitive, which is faithful to the spirit of the method; cure means both protecting, defending, guaranteeing, and giving back or recovering health, or alternatively, alleviating sorrow. The term 'post-education', which Freud sometimes uses, has its merits, but the term 'cure' reminds us that analytic practice, from the outset, has always and primarily situated itself in the therapeutic field; even the training analysis does not contradict this reality, since its process, when it takes place, reveals the demand for treatment through the quest for meaning. The idea of cure, with the whole range of its ambitions, takes into account the diversity of sufferings and the heterogeneity of pathological organizations. It does not refer to the abstract, negative norm of a non-conflictual state of health, but to the dynamic organization of an Ego, which, by virtue of its instinctual introjections, is capable of elaborating the constitutive conflicts of psychic life. At its most general level, psychoanalytic cure appears as one of the valid solutions that modernity provides for the human sickness that Freud speaks of in *Civilization and its Discontents* (1930): a sickness whose essential manifestation is the particular inaptitude for happiness, even though the quest for it seems to constitute the very mainspring of life.

For Freud, and in the light of the ambiguity of instinctual vicissitudes, cure in psychoanalysis only corresponds, for each person, to a singular libidinal equation translating the relative harmonisation of conflicts, which, beyond their intra-erotic forms (narcissism-object relation, individual-group, restricted group-large group), refers to the radical conflict between the life drives and the death drives.

One can see how the notion of cure as a by-product both leaves the analysand with the task of discovering the singular equation of his desires, the distribution of his investments, and inscribes itself, owing to its very principle, alongside the supremacy of the forces of Eros.[7]

I want to return now to the original postulate according to which cure as a *by-product* implies the functional autonomy of the method. This postulate has gradually revealed its relativity and its precarious status:

 - on the one hand, clinical experience shows that there is no regular proportionality between the depth of the process and its therapeutic effects (given that their evaluation is very difficult);
 - on the other hand, it has revealed the major problem of failures, deteriorations, etc.

It is therefore not easy to distinguish those cases where the employment of the method has not worked from those where what is lacking is results. The entire history of the technique could be read in terms of the twofold effort to make the method more adequate and / or more beneficial.

How can the the different possible 'responses' of the method be characterized? The negative therapeutic reaction provides an example: it shows the complex interference between method and events. What is Freud's approach?

The fact is selected and sifted out from the modes of resistance already listed; this objectification signals a *limit of the method*.

For Freud, the obstacle of this objectification justifies the detour of metapsychological speculation which aims, through a change of perspective, at making the phenomenon more intelligible.

The practical contribution is indirect: the theorization proposes a new interpretive potential which *perhaps* increases the virtual pertinence of the method. This schema shows that the psychoanalytic response of the method to that which calls it into question cannot consist in an applicable technical recipe: it involves a complexification of the analytic function in the service of its functional autonomy. It takes into account the gap between method and result, and brings into play the gap between theory and practice.

This schema is certainly too general; how, in the course of a treatment, does the analyst respond? First of all, no doubt, by an evaluation which concerns the whole history of the treatment, and the processual context against which the phenomenon, the event, stands out; of course, the appreciation of the transferential–counter-transferential relation of the moment is crucial.

In effect, the challenge to the method here concerns, in the first place, the subjective dimension of the psychoanalyst's function. Counter-transferential reactions are grasped through the subjective disturbance of the exercise of this function; the postulate of the method is that this disturbance is potentially utilizable. This postulate clashes with the fact that a characteristic of the phenomenon is to render this utilization provisionally inaccessible. The work of counter-transference thus comes first; but its outcome will often come from an unexpected operation of *après-coup* (*Nachträglichkeit*), or from recourse to secondary listening. What constitutes the analytic value of the response is that its adequacy is bound up—even if in a transgressive mode—with the reference points of the method. This is why the phenomenon of the counter-transference (in its unconscious motivation) can only make sense in reference to a theoretically defined, delimited function. Added to this, in the interanalytic register, is the fact that the theory of the countertransference necessarily involves the indefinite problematization of this function.

Thus the most creative analysts speak of crises of the method, of extreme situations; in doing so, they contribute an experience of counter-transference to the technique which enlarges, on a lesser or greater scale, the basis of the analytic function.

These creative variants form part of the history of the method, with the contradictions and effects of incompatibility to which the current pluralism of the theories of practice bear witness.

The notion of variant is thus relative: what has constituted, at a particular moment, a necessarily transgressive variant in relation to the method, may become part of the foreseeable variations of the complexified method. In the same way, what is variant for a group is only defined in relation to the definition that this group gives of the analytic function. It seems to me that this tension between orthodoxy or orthopraxy and transgression is inevitable; and that it is indispensable to preserve the gap between subject and function which underlies the method's vocation of producing thirdness.

I will just say a word in passing about the variants that may be qualified as defensive. The essential feature about these responses to what challenges the pertinence of the method is a certain renunciation. This renunciation can be selective, provisional, or definitive; it can be partial or total; above all, it can be explicit (for example, suspension during hospitalization) or may be marked by a general change of orientation by the analyst. Thus it may be translated by resorting to advice, reassurance, and support.

What is important, here, for me, is not to consider the necessity, or the pertinence of this change of orientation; nor to approach the question of a mixture of genres which is at the centre of the problem of the psychoanalytic psychotherapies.

I simply want to point out that these variants, from the moment they confirm a certain inadequacy of the method, also have the effect of undermining what constitutes one of its strengths, namely, the coherent continuity of its employment. The ever-present risk, as I have said, is to give up the interpretive perspective for the uncertain alternative of fine-sounding words. A sign of the regressive value of this change of orientation is that it is often designated as 'psychotherapeutic'. Certainly, as I have indicated, the designated procedures are one of the characteristics of psychoanalytic psychotherapies. But it is still true that speaking of a psychotherapeutic reorientation can suggest that support, advice, and so on, because they are a sign of the analyst's caring attitude, are *ipso facto* therapeutic, while interpretation is not.

Such disdain is secretly sustained by the confusion arising from the false split between psychoanalysis and psychoanalytic psychotherapies. Hence the importance of stressing the fact that the postulate of an effect of cure is inherent to every analytic project; the deployment of the complex issues involved in the cure as a by-product shows that they are at work at the very heart of the practice of the method.

II. Concerning psychoanalytic psychotherapies

The current situation requires the analytic movement as a whole to re-examine its status (Israel, 1999). Beyond the oppositions linked to the politics of psychoanalysis, and to the diversity of the professional and teaching positions, I would like to try and understand what the methodological issue is that divides analysts with respect to them.

To do this, I will take as my starting-point the double and partially contradictory articulation that characterizes the analytic method.[8]

Its matrix is the pair free association–interpretive *après-coup*. Its correlate is the fundamental postulate of the processual dynamic stemming from the transferential encounter, a dynamic which activates psychic representation *at all its levels*. The first task of the analytic situation and of the analyst is to accompany and share this processual movement. This is why, in order to develop an aptitude for evenly-suspended listening, for the formal regression of thinking, and for the use of his unconscious memory, the analyst must have experienced the transference relationship and the method for himself.

But the analyst's task also implies the mastery, even if relative, of the conditions in which this matrix of shared associative thinking proves to be at once possible, interpretable and beneficial. The method thus brings into play clinical thinking arising from analytic experience and knowledge. This thinking necessarily rests on the objective typical characteristics of the structures and modes of functioning.

Associative thinking and clinical thinking cannot really be dissociated, any more than primary and secondary processes can.[9] The method presupposes their articulation, through mutual opposition and support, but this articulation *varies* according to patients and different moments in the process. This variation concerns the theoretico-practical gap, for regressively deployed associative thinking corresponds to a maximal disjunction between theory and practice (Bion's negative capacity comes to mind here); whereas clinical thinking realizes a certain conjunction between theory and practice (the danger of which should not be overlooked). The variations of this contradictory tension at the heart of the method depend both on patients and working situations. If the processual postulate and associative thinking underlie the principle of the unity of analytic practice, it is for clinical thinking to account for the diversity of the conditions of its utilization.

To echo Marilia Aisenstein's assertion that 'psychoanalytic psychotherapy does not exist', I would like to ask myself *how* it exists. And it should be noted that it exists, primarily, in everyday usage, through what opposes it to psychoanalysis.

When it is a question of beginning an analysis, the virtual pertinence of the method is in general the object of close examination, owing to the constraints and risks that it implies. The intensity of the mutual commitment concretized by the frame implies that the situation involves the presence of two subjects with different but sufficient capacities. The analytic model *stricto sensu* realizes the conjunction between a patient of analysis, an analyst, and the 'standard' analytic situation. The force of attraction, sometimes excessive, of this model arises from the fact that it offers the processual postulate of the method its optimal conditions of operation, conditions under which the process has the best chances of articulating in its development continuity and discontinuity, complexity and intelligibility, unbinding and rebinding, and finally, specific transformations and healing effects. This is why, when it is well-indicated and conducted, psychoanalysis, for the analyst, can only be the best of psychotherapies.

In these optimal conditions, the method centres itself spontaneously on shared associative thinking. Because it has, as it were, *materialized* itself within a frame, and because this frame functions silently, it is as if clinical thinking were suspended; even the emergence of interpretation appears to be caught in the dynamics of the process. Here we are in the logic of the *well-tempered couch*.

The conjunction analytic situation–patient-analyst can scarcely be reduced, however, to this model, owing to the extension of the indications. It seems to me that the weakening of the prior 'fit' which results from this increases proportionately the eventual recourse to clinical thinking, and, consequently, the risks linked to the conjunction between theory and practice. Even when, and because he

finds himself obliged to listen to the patient's manifestations as free
association, the analyst relies more than elsewhere on his clinical
knowledge and the principles of his method. In spite of—and thanks
to—the variation of the equilibrium between associative thinking
and clinical thinking, the method remains, as I pointed out earlier,
centred on the maximal deployment of the processual postulate.

The field of psychoanalytic psychotherapy looks quite different:
the heterogeneity of the patients is greater in it because the criteria
of indication are more approximate; they are less demanding as well,
because the mutual commitment is materialized in a less intense
working situation. It is thus almost impossible to identify a conjunction of the prior fit that is comparable to the one that is operative in the
standard analytic situation. The description of types of psychotherapies is made with reference to disparate factors: sometimes the setting; sometimes the patients' modes of functioning (psychosomatic,
borderline, adolescents, etc.); sometimes the modes of intervention
(support, clarification, confrontation, etc.); and sometimes targeting
the aim (current conflict, corrective emotional experience, etc.).

These descriptions bear witness to considerable clinical experience which is utilizable up to a certain point. Ultimately, what seems
to constitute the unity of this loose conglomeration is only the negative conjunction which links an unanalyzable patient, an analyst who
has more or less given way with regard to the method, and a reduced
working situation. This negative conjunction no doubt nourishes the
pejorative attitude which often exists towards psychoanalytic psychotherapies. This tendency goes hand in hand with an idealization of the
model of the analytic situation which could, as we have seen, make us
forget the therapeutic vocation of every psychoanalytic encounter.

Two characteristics are found constantly in the methodology of
psychoanalytic psychotherapies:

1. The reduction of the working situation, whether it concerns the
   number or rhythm of the sessions or the formal specificity of the
   frame—face-to-face rather than the couch.[10] This reduced frame
   belongs to the instruments of the method; it is obviously postulated that it has an effect on the processual phenomena and the
   mode of the analyst's response.
2. The recommendation of pre-adequate modes of action faced with
   typical modes of functioning. These recommendations do not

have the same status as the variants mentioned above, which claimed to be exclusively in the service of the processual perspective; here, they readily claim to trace *in advance* the path that must be followed in order to arrive at a predetermined aim. As a general rule, they are not concerned with how they are linked to the matrix of the method. They seem to translate the demand for a direct use of clinical knowledge, which makes one think of Ferenczi's abrupt formula in his correspondence with Freud during the conflict of 1924: 'What we attempted was only an attempt to use the knowledge already gleaned more energetically in technique, for once' (Freud-Ferenczi, 2000, p. 121).[11]

There is a link between the use of the reduced frame and the tendency to make such recommendations. The use of knowledge is a sign of the temporary or permanent prevalence of clinical thinking over associative thinking. This link is confirmed indirectly by the reactions of the analytic institution towards the delicate problem raised by the training of non analyst practitioners in psychoanalytic psychotherapy.

The justification for such training is, on the face of it, that these practitioners would not use the standard analytic situation; consequently, they do not need to go through the personal experience which is at the heart of the training of analysts.[12] The use of the reduced frame would thus make the mode of associative thinking characteristic of the analyst's functioning in the session contingent. Analysts who support this position are in conflict within the psychoanalytic institution with those who consider that only an analyst can conduct a psychoanalytic psychotherapy.

Of course, analytic training cannot be reduced to the experience of personal analysis—second fundamental rule—and it must integrate the field of clinical thinking in the broadest sense. The risk exists that an analyst trained for the analytic situation alone is unaware not only of the difficulties of patients who do not fall within its scope, but also of the relative specificity of the use of the reduced frame. For analysts who are against such training, it is not that they are unaware of the methodological implications of the reduced frame, but that they wish to stress that the particular difficulty in it of supporting and optimizing the processual postulate of associative thinking, as well as the subsequent tendency to make a purely counter-transferential use of clinical thinking, make analytic training even more necessary.

This brings me back, then, to the need to think simultaneously about the unity and the diversity of analytic treatments. The received opposition between psychoanalysis and psychoanalytic psychotherapy has no doubt become more troublesome than useful. The unifying reference to analytic work is a current attempt to go beyond it: the danger is to aggravate the tendency towards a levelling of working situations to the detriment of the most demanding of them. The evolution of the offer and demand has resulted in two intersecting phenomena: on the one hand, many analysts propose the analytic situation to extreme patients; on the other, many potential patients refuse any intensive commitment and only accept a reduced frame.

Consequently, the chosen frame depends on a more uncertain 'prior fit', and results more often from a pure compromise of feasibility. It has thus become more necessary to take into consideration, in as precise and nuanced a manner as possible, the effect of the working situation on the potentialities of the process and on the internal equilibrium of the method employed.

III. Why a logic of the site?

The unifying reference to psychoanalytic work assumes that it is up to the analyst to make sure that, for each patient, the process is optimized. But this perspective may not take sufficient account of the complexity of the relations that are formed between the patient, the analyst, and the plural expectations of the method.

To what extent does the notion of the site prove useful when it is a case of accounting for the diversity of psychoanalytic treatments? The site is not the setting, but it almost inevitably has to be grasped via this element—at once the most material and conventional—especially as its choice usually occurs before the analysis begins. However, the notion of site implies not exploring the consequences of this choice in an isolated or univocal manner, but considering them through their correlations with the configuration which assures the functional coherence of the whole, that is to say, *the logic of the site*.

To take a minimal and ordinary example: the change from the armchair to the couch or even simply the change from one to two sessions a week in the face-to-face setting, is accompanied by a modification of the basis of the processual postulate, and of the analytic function. If the setting of the standard analytic situation represented metonymically, and to an excessive degree, the whole of the method, it is because it seemed, owing to an adequate number of weekly sessions and the lying position, to be structurally linked to the *radical* application of the fundamental rule.

Thus, the notion of site demands that the implications of a decision about the frame—whether or not it results from a technical choice—be considered from the angle of this configuration whose virtual functional coherence constitutes *the logic of the site*. The site results, then, from a selective division of the means of the method, which marks the nature of the processual postulate and the basis of the analytic function. The transition from the face-to-face situation to the couch-armchair position, for example, makes such an effect manifest. Even the change from one session to two sessions a week, in the face-to-face position, presupposes a similar modification, even if it is minimal and almost imperceptible.

The logic of the site seems to be an objective phenomenon that is external to the protagonists, stemming from the clinical experience of typical structures. If we examine it more closely, it appears to be duplicated by the process.

- On the one hand, the frame is assumed to have an effect on the nature and organization of the processual phenomena. Indeed it is this assumption that makes its choice important, even if this effect is very difficult to foresee and objectivize.[13] These are the characteristics of the processual phenomena, and, in particular, of the manifestations of the transference, which will *elicit* a certain kind of response from the analyst.
- On the other hand, however, the decision concerning the frame, particularly if it is a technical choice, implies a certain *anticipation* in the analyst, which inevitably marks his listening and his interventions in such a way that that they will have their own effect on the process.

From the first perspective, and once the frame has been objectivized, it is the process that modifies the analyst's function; from the second, it is the site, as a modality of the analyst's clinical thinking, which modulates the process. The two perspectives can scarcely be distinguished in the processual movement, so that the notion of site presents an ambiguity whereby it sometimes includes the function of the analyst and sometimes is included in it in the form of an *operative idea* in the analyst's mind. The functional logic of the site presents itself both as an objective causality and as an effect of the link, marked by subjectivity, between the psychoanalyst and his/the method.

The logic of the site is thus *probabilistic*, an effect and sign of the relative autonomy of the method and its mediating position between the patient and the analyst. It shows simultaneously that the incidence of the site is unavoidable and that it does not have the value of a causal determinism, since, ultimately, it is unforeseeable events which will give the encounter its meaning.

Being present in a more or less preconscious manner in the analyst's mind, the logic of the site should only function as an expectant idea open to modification. It forms part of the basis that is necessary for anticipating the operation of *après-coup* and thus participates in the methodological paradox of confounded prediction and prescribed surprise.

Would it be possible to understand its logic for each of the sites that are organized in relation to the diverse working situations in the field of psychoanalytic practice? For this to be possible, each of them would have to present sufficiently typical characteristics. Every site could then be described according to the specificity—however relative and approximate—of its logic. Their necessary comparison could escape any kind of hierarchical perspective since each one would have the drawbacks of its advantages, its *shadow;*[14] each would permit/produce its process and its counter-process,[15] including the analytic site in spite of its value as a paradigm.

These objective typical characteristics stand out quite naturally in the case of sites whose specific object (child, family, group), the introduction of a particular form of mediation (play, drawing, psychodrama, relaxation, etc.) have made a transposition of the method necessary.[16] Making them explicit helps one to appreciate how the fundamental elements of the method are configured according to a specific logic; it is this logic which makes the site *a priori* preferentially suitable for this or that type of patient (for example, psychodrama for patients who have difficulties of representation).

The problem of differentiation is posed much more vaguely in the case of sites which are organized around the gradient of settings that an analyst is in a position to propose from the therapeutic consultation to five weekly sessions on the couch. It is clear that such a gradient is translated by discontinuities that are too tenuous for it to be possible to make them correspond to logics that are even remotely specific. More precisely, it seems that the difference between the sites is too slight not to be covered over or masked in their everyday use by the differences that the diversity of the patients reveal in their use of one and the same site. This is one of the reasons why clinical thinking so readily makes recommendations directly concerning typical forms of psychic functioning; or alternatively, becomes fixed on the schematic opposition between psychoanalysis and psychotherapy. And yet, clinical research shows that the exploration of this issue is fruitful.

To illustrate this, I am going to take the easily identifiable example of the site which is organized around the weekly face-to-face session.

Let me note right away that there is a functional correlation between the face-to-face situation and the weekly session. I also note that this setting does not differ from that of any other meeting: the analyst will no doubt have to signify more explicitly the psychoanalytic dimension of the work that is going to be undertaken.

The interest of the face-to-face situation has been explored in detail, but an element of opaqueness still remains: it maintains the exchange or avoidance of eye contact; it integrates within the mutual communication facial expressions, gestures, postures, with the advantages and disadvantages that this implies; the privilege of speech in the lying position disappears, but the discourse is often accompanied emotionally in a more noticeable way. The face-to-face situation tends to support the relationship to the analyst *in person*: there is scarcely any opportunity for his perception and representation to become dissociated. Now, it is against the background of their disjunction that the experience of their temporary confusion confers on transferential projection its particular consistency at the same time as its interpretability. The face-to-face situation is thus less favourable for understanding the transference as such, which elucidates, but does not justify, the old recommendation to use the transference without interpreting it. However, an interpretation of the transference runs the increased risk of being received as a rectification of the projection. Freud's formula (1913, p. 139), 'One must wait until the transference has become a resistance' is particularly relevant here.

The only incidence of the face-to-face situation is that it deeply modifies the nature of the processual postulate: a transference interpretation, even if it is identical in content and form, is neither given nor received in the same way as in the analytic situation. Elements such as friendly neutrality and reserved silence have to be signified differently against the background of more manifest affective support.

The radical application of the fundamental rule is rarely possible. There can be no question, of course, of abandoning free association, but this *tends* naturally to assume the initial form of the procedure used for investigating an object brought by the patient at the beginning of the session. This object, *already there,* may be a dream, a traumatic memory, etc., but it turns out very often to be a scene from daily life concerning which the patient expects to receive some *practical*[17] elucidation.

These phenomena are linked to the uniqueness of the session: unlike the analytic site where each session has its own process but will be 'followed up' in the weekly sequence, the process of the single session, which is particularly invested, encourages the realization of a sample of analysis that has its own pertinence; a signifying closure will be welcome, constituting 'food' for the week.

The analytic function is thus affected: even if the analyst tries to preserve the associative functioning and the operation of *après-coup,* he does not have the same temporality at his disposal as in the analytic site where all the detours and repetitions are assumed not only to be inevitable but necessary, owing to the principle of working-through resistances. Here, the analyst's relation to the handling of the duration of the session is modified: the analyst is led to intervene more often, and his decisions to intervene or interpret are taken more quickly, in a processual context that is more uncertain; he does not always have time to elaborate his countertransferential movements so that, making a virtue out of necessity, he uses them readily *in statu nascendi, verging on acting out.* The logic of the site legitimates the role played by the personal equation of the analyst, which appears to be both the reverse side and the complement of the direct use of his knowledge. Noting that the logic of the site allows one to be less finicky about the effects of suggestion does not mean that it promotes them.

The logic of the site has to make do with the shortcomings of the processual contextualization; it thus relies on the possibility of anticipating trajectories and supports the *principle of the short cut*. It is true that in *Analysis Terminable and Interminable* (1937), Freud remarks on the general failure of attempts to shorten analysis but, as soon as he had given up the idea of a process which leads to natural end, he opened up the question of *incomplete* analysis, of the incompleteness of every analysis. It is possible to answer this question from the standpoint of a sufficient coherence of the processual trajectory proceeding from an *optimal utilization of the site*—an optimization that is an essential aspect of the site.

This illustration shows, it seems to me, that it is possible to explore the logic of the site while *suspending* the crucial issue of its singular, and ultimately unpredictable, use by the patient. It also shows that the logic of the site does not involve a deliberate procedure on the analyst's part, but proceeds in a quasi-automatic way; it thus relates to a regulation stemming from a functional coherence which organizes itself processually.

Even if it proves incapable of differentiating precisely the logics of sites organized in relation to frames that are very similar, clinical research should not abandon the exploration of this question.

Notes

1. Analytic psychotherapies, formerly PIP, i.e. 'Psychoanalytically Inspired Psychotherapies' (René Held).
2. There exists a 'standard working situation' for all patients, whereas the notion of a 'standard process' (*cure type*) is debatable.
3. There is no medical monopoly. As far as psychotherapy is concerned, its practice is open to clinical psychologists. The current debate about a status, or label, underlines the telescoping of technical, corporatist, and financial issues, as well as those of public protection, which are involved.
4. See Addendum 'Constraint of method and/or constraint of finality'.
5. See *Revue française de psychanalyse*, vol. 64, 5, 2000, 'L'idéal transmis', Congress for French-Speaking Psychoanalysts in Montreal, in particular J.-L. Donnet; 'Ils ne mourront pas tous ...'
6. In the minefield of training analysis, the institutional desire for a 'complete' analysis gave rise to the somewhat totalitarian idea that the analyst should be a completely 'cured' analysand, that is to say,

here, normalised. It can be considered that currently, in France, the more modest idea of the 'personal' analysis prevails, that is, of an analysis whose most assured criterion of success would be to find one's way and one's own temporality, outside the institution. Hence the valorization of the process as such, even if it remains clear that the analysis of an eventual future analyst is an analysis *that will be attested to* in one way or another.

7. I am thus not in complete agreement with N. Zaltzman when she criticizes the notion of cure (recovery) as a by-product, considering that analytic cure is inherent to the process and thus indistinguishable from specific psychic transformations. This point of view makes it necessary to postulate that these transformations have a natural extension in a 'civilizing' effect on the patient's family circle. This clinical reality is undeniable, and it is present, moreover, in certain indications (for example, subjects who come to analysis because of the problem that the parental function poses them, the fear of transmitting their unconscious conflicts). But it cannot be generalized, since the individual cure does not necessarily fit in with this general line of thinking. Nevertheless, as soon as the supremacy of Eros is involved, is it not legitimate to link, as N. Zaltzman does, the analytic process and the cultural process through the notion of *Kulturarbeit*? In one sense, this is what Freud does in *Civilization and its Discontents*, by designating the individual and collective processes as instinctual in nature, which implies, ultimately, that what is at stake in them is the struggle between the two groups of drives, Eros and the death drives. However, Freud stresses the relative antagonism of the two processes. I think it is necessary to think about how the analytic process, which is eminently individual, works in favour of reducing this antagonism (notably via the sublimatory valency of the method), while preserving its relative autonomy; especially as the *Kulturarbeit* of the individual is better known, and in any case more accessible to psychoanalysis, than in the cultural process where, Freud stresses, a satisfactory equilibrium is impossible because the menace posed by the death drive and primary hostility against civilization is counterbalanced by the unreasonable excesses of Eros. It will be recalled that Freud designates the sickness of culture as incurable, if not unanalyzable, or curable by the prophet which he refuses to be. The question posed by N. Zaltzman concerns the metapsychological coincidence between the psychization of the instinctual drive and the socialization of the psyche.

8. See Chapter 1 'From the Fundamental Rule to the Analyzing Situation'.
9. This highlights the importance of tertiary processes (A. Green) in the analyst's mode of functioning. I would also point out that A. Green includes under the term clinical thinking the totality of that which is related to analytic thinking brought into play in clinical practice (see *Psychoanalysis: a paradigm for clinical thinking*, London: Free Association Books, 2002).
10. This reduction is found everywhere, but it is relative to what, for an analyst or a group of analysts, defines the standard analytic situation. In France, where psychoanalysis implies three/four sessions per week on the couch, psychotherapy usually refers to a weekly (or twice weekly, face-to-face session). In London, where the analytic standard is five sessions, three sessions, even on the couch, is called psychotherapy.
11. The paradigm at the time being the direct reference to the trauma of birth (Rank), which greatly troubled Freud, before he compared this method to that of a fireman who claims to put out a fire by removing the overturned lamp that started it.
12. The institutions concerned are themselves divided on this subject. Some require, others recommend, a form of personal experience: but the definition of its setting reduplicates the question.
13. It has been pointed out, not without reason, that there is something paradoxical in the tendency to propose a less intensive setting while the patient presents greater difficulties. This shows that the choice of the setting is partly dependent on the countertransference; I would prefer to say that the countertransferential capacity is part of the site.
14. In my critique of Lacanian acted scansion (Donnet, 1995), I pointed out that the classical setting—notably, the fixed duration of sessions—has its shadow. But it remains analyzable retrospectively, whereas acted scansion becomes an act that has succeeded in advance, which renders the principle of its interpretive value useless.
15. See *Psychothérapies psychanalytiques*, Paris, PUF, 'Monographies de la Revue Française de Psychanalyse', 1998. This collection of articles illustrates convincingly the diversity of the sites.
16. I am not taking into consideration here the very variable distance that this transposition introduces in relation to the paradigm of the standard analytic situation.
17. The increased use of the reduced setting and the increasing frequency of statements like 'I want to work on my mother', etc., can be linked.

References

Aisenstein, M. (2001). 'Psychoanalytic psychotherapy does not exist'. In *Psychoanalysis and Psychotherapy: the Controversies and the Future* (chapter 2). London: Karnac Books, 2001.

Donnet, J.-L. (1995). *Le divan bien-tempéré*. Paris : Presses Universitaires de France.

Freud, S. (1900). *The Interpretation of Dreams. SE*, 4 and 5.

Freud, S. (1901). *The Psychopathology of Everyday Life. SE*, 6.

Freud, S. (1905). *Three Essays on the Theory of Sexuality. SE*, 7.

Freud, S. (1905). *Jokes and their Relation to the Unconscious. SE*, 8.

Freud, S. (1913). *On Beginning the Treatment. SE*, 12.

Freud, S. (1923 [1922]). *Two Encaeclopaedia Articles. SE*, 18.

Freud, S. (1926). *The Question of Lay Analysis. SE*, 20.

Freud, S. (1930). *Civilization and its Discontents. SE*, 21.

Freud, S. (1937). *Analysis Terminable and Interminable. SE*, 23.

Freud, S. & Ferenczi, S. (2000). *The Correspondence of Sigmund Freud and Sandor Ferenczi, vol 3 (1923–1933)*, trans. P. Hoffer. Cambridge (Mass.): Harvard University Press.

Israel, P. (1999). 'La psychanalyse et la psychothérapie analytique', *IPA Letter*, vol. 8, 1, January 1999, pp. 14–18.

Zaltzmann, N. (2000). *De la guérison psychanalytique*. Paris : Presses Universitaires de France, 'Épîtres'.

Constraint of method and/or constraint of finality

I think it would be interesting to return to a fragment of an article (Donnet, 1989) in which I discussed two points of Tzvetan Todorov's (1977)[1] theory of the symbol.

1. With regard to symbolic language, Todorov rejects the point of view that all discourse is symbolic. He defends the duality of a direct, immediately understood discourse, and of a discourse which *calls for* interpretation. So he refers, as if to an essential criterion, to the *feeling of the 'language user'*. It seemed to me that the subjective character of this criterion could be compared with an essential psychoanalytic concern: the *feeling of the 'couch user'*. In the light of this analogy, it was interesting to examine the duality Todorov has identified concerning the intra- or extra-textual indices underlying the decision to interpret. As far as the couch user is concerned, this decision is a function of the presumed admissibility of the interpretation. In the initial logic of the fundamental rule, the *Einfall*, as an *involuntary thought*, naturally appeared to be a fragment of symbolic discourse that was linked to a return of the repressed and that required interpretation.

The extension of the rule to the entire session effaces this conventional discrimination and makes the recognition of the intra-
textual indices which *justify* interpretation more complex, so that
the extra-textual conditions—the limits of the frame—designate
every discourse as being potentially interpretable, as saying
something other than what it says. The possibility thus arises of
a simultaneous translation and the risk of a pre-coded interpretation, of hermeneutics. The reference to the feeling of the couch
user—that is, of the analysand—thus remains an essential reference. The 'situation analysis'[2] designates in particular the appropriation of the analytic process whereby the analysand *grants* the
analyst the freedom to hear him associatively, that is to say, to
hear everything he says *as* free association. I am thinking here, for
example, of Freud's (1925) article on negation in which he writes:
'we take the liberty of disregarding the negation' (p. 235). This
liberty must be *used* by the analyst, but it will only acquire meaning by becoming the rule of a shared interplay.

2. Considering the general principles of the major interpretive
   strategies—biblical exegesis, historical materialism, structuralism,
   psychoanalysis—Todorov poses that their procedure is faced
   with an unavoidable alternative and choice: they have to
   choose between constraint of method and constraint of finality.
   Thus historical materialism has a pre-established finality—the
   confirmation of its laws—but has to invent a rigorous path to
   achieve it. On the contrary, structuralism, which sets itself no
   prior finality, accepts a defined methodology.

   According to Todorov, psychoanalysis has a pre-established
   finality—for example, rediscovering the Oedipus complex, infantile sexuality, etc.—and discovers the paths which lead there. In
   certain respects, Todorov's assertion might be justified, but it has
   also raised many objections. Above all, the alternative itself did
   not seem to correspond to the specific characteristics of *analytic
   practice*; and, primarily, to the tension between transferential
   actualization and the feeling of the couch user—a tension that
   involves the whole issue of resistance and of *'making sense'*. In fact,
   it is important to emphasize that the analytic method implies an
   essential oscillation between ends and means. There is no *means*
   which, in a given processual context, cannot appear as a finality,
   a preliminary or provisional *result*. For example, the telling of a

dream was understood by Freud as a privileged means, a royal road, for discovering unconscious desire. But the eventual emergence of a dream constitutes an effect of the analytic work: a sign of a transformation of the psychic functioning and a desirable *result* in a patient who hitherto had not dreamed. Similar remarks could be made concerning processual phenomena as a whole. The Oedipus complex does not present itself as an ensemble of repressed wishes, an object to be reconstituted in the sense of the archeological metaphor used by Freud; its historical-prehistorical reality cannot be dissociated from its value as a processual psychic organizer of the transference neurosis, including the counter-transferential involvement, and thus the theoretical support of the analyst. Basically, Todorov's inquiry concerns the operation of the function of the third in analytic work, a function whose vicissitudes accompany the transference regression.

The distinction between ends and means proves problematic in the field of psychoanalysis, and the Freudian postulate of the disjunction between the initiation of the method and the hoped-for recovery remains a crucial reference. In function of this postulate, recovery (or cure) is an *additional benefit*, the mediate, indirect effect of the analytic work. In this sense, one could point out to Todorov that psychoanalysis does not assign any prior finality, while respecting a strict discipline of means. On the other hand, the autonomy of the method implies an intimate weaving between the utilization of these means and the specific psychic transformations which it induces. This weaving, which blurs the distinction between ends and means, stems from the concomitance between the production of transference and its interpretation.

The autonomy of the method remains, however, a guarantee of the consistency of the effects of recovery. One can say that, for the analyst—and for the analysand—'qui veut la fin veut les moyens'[3] acquires a particularly rigorous meaning.

Notes

1. See also, by the same author, *Symbolisme et interpretation*, Paris, Le Seuil, 1978.
2. Translator's note: The French here is 'analytique de situation' (like 'situation comedy').

3. Translator's note: 'he who wants the ends, wants the means', a formulation stressing the *value of the means* which give value to the ends, which is clearly different from the expression the 'ends justify the means'.

References

Donnet, J.L. (1989). 'Symbolisation et règle fondamentale, le faire sens'. In *Revue française de Psychanalyse*, reporter A. Gibeault, vol. 53, 6.

Freud, S. (1925). 'Negation'. *S.E. 19*: 233–239.

Todorov, T. (1977). *Théories du symbole*. Paris : Le Seuil.

Psychoanalytic encounter
and consultation

(I) I am using the term 'encounter' here to designate what takes place between someone who is seeking analysis and the analyst he/ she decides to consult, i.e., from the very first contact to the mutual agreement on beginning, or not beginning, an analysis. Thus defined, the encounter may consist in one or several interviews. I think it is interesting to try and identify how the question of the beginning, which comprises the ambiguities already mentioned, is posed.

(II) For many analysts, the psychoanalysis of a subject coincides with the very opening of the encounter, posed as *always already* psychoanalytic. Does the psychoanalyst not *immediately* assume his position, activating his mode of listening and offering it to the spontaneity of an associative discourse? Is he not in a position to confer on his virtual engagement or commitment a subjectivized dimension, with the countertransferential involvement that is an essential motivating factor of it? Is he not in a position to guarantee the continuity of his support for the transferential movement that is present or solicited from the outset?

It is very true that, in some cases, the initial encounter leads so naturally into the beginning of a treatment, within a framework easily agreed upon, that it seems, retrospectively, to have been its indisputable point of departure, without the slightest discontinuity. It is understandable that this so *purely* analytic form of beginning functions as a model. The risks of idealizing it need to be considered though: a striking example, of which I have had repeated experience, is the irrational hostility which seems to be its correlate with regard to the *psychoanalytic consultation,* that is, the encounter between an analyst who is excluded *a priori* from any subsequent involvement and someone seeking analysis who is duly aware of this. This is the situation that is operative institutionally in the functioning of the CCTP,[1] but, like many others, I also have experience of this in private practice when I accept to see someone who still wants a consultation with me even after I have informed them that I will not be available thereafter. I do not intend here to return to the unquestionable but limited disadvantages, any more than to the particular interest, of such an encounter. The hostility that it arouses can be explained, in fact, by the denial of the consultative dimension present in every encounter, and even furtively, in the one mentioned above.

(III) I will make the most crucial point first: it is wrong to assimilate the analyst's mode of listening during the encounter with what it can be during a session. How can one forget that, in the encounter, listening remains informed by the *issue of refusal*: the virtual patient's words are capable of provoking in the analyst the decision to refuse to take him/her on; whereas, once he has taken the person on, assuming fully his function and responsibility as an analyst, an eventual affective movement of refusal will be no more than an indication of the counter-transferential function. Unless one excludes in advance and, as a matter of principle, the possibility of a refusal, it is impossible to contend that the analyst is from the outset really in the position of analyst: the encounter *is not* psychoanalytic; it can become so when the refusal has been eliminated. In different, more objectivizing terms, it could be said that it constitutes an *experimental treatment,* with the ambiguity and even the sense of uneasiness that this involves, which we feel so clearly now with regard to the Freudian proposition of a trial psychoanalysis of a few months.

The encounter is thus, on both sides, an experiment which must take the time it needs, but should be as short as possible; it is diversely, but structurally marked by the decision, whatever it may be, which *inevitably* constitutes its term, its point of closure.

Several remarks need to be made concerning this decision, in order to emphasize that it will have to take into account and to integrate *heterogeneous* registers of reality:

- This decision on the analyst's part implies, even minimally, an evaluation, that is, the use of his clinical experience and of the relative prediction that it permits. The reference to subjective experience and the identification of a counter-transferential involvement are part of this phase of objectification. It is not because it can occur very early on, or go almost unnoticed, that its necessity should be overlooked. I do not mean to suggest that the analyst's decision proceeds from the objectivity of clinical knowledge; I simply want to point out that a consultative dimension is inherent to the encounter, that it brings into play the tertiary reference to established psychoanalysis.
- A second remark is that the decision which marks the end of the encounter will have succeeded in combining, in one way or another, three distinct issues: the first is that of a reciprocal co-optation which occurs on the terrain of the intersubjective relationship; the second concerns the working framework agreed upon, the recommendation of which is the analyst's responsibility; and the third issue concerns feasibility, and especially the financial agreement, the burden of which we are all familiar with.

Without entering into the diversity of the encounters, I will just point out that these three issues interfere with each other, and that the moment when they are put forward for discussion in the encounter has an effect on the very process. It is neither possible nor desirable to program the timing of these moments, and this is why it quite often happens that their interference is psychoanalytically burdensome: for example, at the end of interviews that have led clearly to a precise and common project, the financial question can suddenly turn out to be an insurmountable obstacle, making it necessary to consider another address. Daily practice thus makes it impossible to privilege the encounter in which the option of the frame and the financial agreement have prolonged the reciprocal cooptation as the only one that is psychoanalytically valid. There is no reason to overestimate the fact that the first analyst encountered will be the one with whom the analysis will be undertaken: such an overestimation evokes the taboo of virginity. Clinical experience shows that when several analysts have been encountered, their personalities are generally metabolized into the figures of the transferential family romance. Perhaps it is necessary, in a truly Freudian way, to point out that, after all, it is psychoanalysis—its method—that the subject encounters through the analyst.

(IV) The initial encounter takes place, then, in a particular site that is provisional and marked by the possibility of an eventual refusal, from whichever side it comes, as well as by the forthcoming decision. The logic of the encounter implies, consequently, a specific conflictuality for the analyst, but it has its equivalent for the person who is consulting:

- on the one hand, the initiation of an experimental situation which imitates the analytic situation, tends to lead to the emergence, through a suspension of the purposive aim, of the beginning of a process which manifests the 'fit' between the virtual patient's psychic functioning and the analytic method, and *vice-versa*;[2]
- on the other hand, however, the analyst remains more or less concerned by his anticipation of the approaching decision. Of course, with some people seeking analysis the tension between these two registers is weak, as it seems quite natural for them to go through the experiment and mutual evaluation, before coming to a decision. But, very often, the individual seeking analysis seems to suggest that he needs to have some degree of assurance about the response in order to be able to speak about himself at all.

It is clear that the ambiguity of the encounter cannot be eliminated, and the complexity of the following question about the beginnings is found in the extreme diversity of its realizations: when and how does the encounter become psychoanalytic? I would be tempted to emphasize two contrasting poles:

- one corresponds to the situation described at the outset, in which the decision to institute the treatment simply confirms the beginning of a process born of and through the encounter, which will

then continue in and through the sessions. *We will begin because we have already begun, so that it may continue;*
- at the other pole, the gamble implied by the decision is more uncertain, the indication is posed at a distance from what has happened during the encounter and rests on a mediate evaluation. The project is based primarily on the dynamic specific to the institution of the setting, the utilization of the site, the handling of the duration: *We will begin because it has not begun, so that it may begin.*

In the gap between these two poles, we can discern how the encounter is a quest for processual meaning, but also, simultaneously, a quest for a frame. This brings us back to the necessity of thinking at one and the same time about the disjunction and conjunction between the processual temporalization and the spatio-temporal frame.

Notes

1. 'Centre de consultation et de traitement psychanalytique Jean Favreau', attached to the Paris Psychoanalytic Society.
2. In French sailing terminology, *'rencontrer'* (as an "intransitive verb") is the manoeuvre whereby a ship which is berthing (or coming alongside another ship) takes a wide or rounded approach to cushion the inevitable bump or shock. By analogy, I want to suggest that in the encounter conceived of as a trial, the shock implied by the consistency of the method goes hand in hand with a flexible, 'rounded out' approach, indicating an elasticity that is particularly necessary here. The dialectic of this fit confers on the unfolding of the meeting its most necessary character, from which will result both the most precise evaluation and, if needs be, the reciprocal conviction that the game is worth the candle.

PART II

The specter-spectrum of the superego

The French edition of *The Analyzing Situation* contains studies centred on the topographical, economic, and, above
all, dynamic dimensions of the said situation: for example,
I explore the new 'royal road' of Freudian *agieren* ('enactment')
by focusing on the specific relations that transferential regression
confers on enacting speech; I also discuss the question of the links
between working-through and silence, the silence of an intra-psychic
latency that is necessary for the symbolizing operation of *après-coup*,
as well as the general problem of the destiny of the transference as
such, in its impersonal register, beyond the analytic object-relation.
But these chapters seemed to me rather too dense and closely linked
to the French semantic context; and so I thought it preferable, in a
book destined for English-speaking readers, to complete the first
part with chapters less centred on the analytic working situation.

So I have chosen four studies that have been well received in
France, the writing of which involved me in a particularly subjective
way. I noticed retrospectively that they were all deeply concerned
with the problematic of the Superego; this was scarcely surprising
since, in the book that I devoted to this theme thirteen years ago

(Donnet, 1995), the Freudian Superego had seemed to me to be a veritable 'site', whose exploration raised more unfathomable questions than clear answers. The studies presented here are an extension of my earlier attempts to identify Freud's difficulties with regard to an agency which nonetheless constitutes, in my judgement, the essential key to the 'metapsychological turning-point of the 1920's'. In contrast to the post-Freudian theorizations which, in an often heuristic manner, it is true, have sought to turn it into a functional concept by erasing certain Freudian inconsistencies, I have gradually persuaded myself that these contradictions were related to precious ambiguities which are the reflection of its essential paradoxical nature. If one seeks to avoid the risk of reducing the Superego to the figure of the policeman which it often has in the 'puppet show' of the agencies, it is perhaps worth preserving its position of speculative ferment, of a border-concept between the individual and culture, as the drive is between the body and the psyche.

I have retained, as a conclusion to this book, the text which also constitutes the last chapter of the French edition ('A Child Is Being Talked About'), whose title echoes Freud's famous article 'A Child Is Being Beaten'. It is a very old text, dating back to 1976, reflecting a time when reading Lacan led me to take into account in a privileged, if not exclusive manner, the role of language in the structuring of the human subject; but, first and foremost, I wrote it while thinking about a screen-memory in my own analysis, whose crucial value I have since been able to verify in innumerable clinical configurations.

CHAPTER FIVE

Lord Jim or the shame of living[1]

ord Jim (1900) is first and foremost a tale of misfortune at sea
and of lost honour. The second part of the novel evokes the
hero's glorious redemption, but his tragic end confirms the self-
destructive dimension of his Ideal. "Lord Jim's" destiny thus assumes
the demonic character that is linked to the compulsion to repeat. I
will only concern myself here with the true/false shipwreck of the
Patna, which is at the origin of Jim's narcissistic shipwreck. The real
event derives its significance from an effect of the operation of *après-
coup* (*Nachträglichkeit*), in the authentically Freudian sense of the term.
To render this effect of *après-coup* in such a way that it is operative
in the narrative of the action, Conrad resorts to a very oblique and
complicated construction whose function goes well beyond the "suspense" that it maintains: it turns out, in fact, that it underlies the very
consistency of the narrative action and the issues which motivate it
subjectively in its protagonists. I will show this through the introduction into the story of the narrator-actor Marlow. First, though, I must
summarize for the reader the episode of the *Patna*.

Jim, who is 24-years-old and has obtained his master's certificate,
has been employed as first mate on board an old steamer whose

captain is a genuine rogue. The *Patna* is transporting eight hundred pilgrims from Asia to the Mecca in Arabia. After colliding with a wreck during the night, in the middle of the Indian Ocean, a major leak occurs at the front of the boat, and it dips its head. The state of the sheet of old iron, which is all that is keeping the sea from rushing in, tells Jim, who has gone forward to inspect it, that the ship is on the point of sinking at any moment. There are only enough boats for a part of the sleeping human cargo, and if the alert is given it will trigger uncontrollable panic, which will not only be useless but fatal. So Jim feels totally helpless. However, the captain and the other three white members of the crew discretely set about launching one of the lifeboats with a view to escaping in it. Jim turns away from them with scornful horror, and, stuck in a position of passive heroism, in conformity with the requisite conduct of Navy officers, prepares himself to go down with the ship and its passengers. From the lifeboat which is preparing to draw away from the ship, increasingly pressing calls to jump are heard; in fact they are addressed to a sailor who has stayed on board and who has suffered a sudden, deadly heart attack. But, as the boat moves away from the ship, Jim finds that he has in fact jumped.

The first phase of the "traumatic" event thus appears to be the sudden actualization of a tragic dilemma between the duty of dying and the desire to live. Faced with this conflict Jim *impulsively* betrays the option of acting in conformity with the ideal with which he has hitherto seemingly been entirely identified. There is a radical contrast—described in unforgettable detail—between the "others" (the captain and the members of the crew) for whom self-preservation prevails over any other consideration, and Jim who has long been filled with heroic fantasies. So the 'leap' into the boat is an isolated case of *acting out* that cannot be integrated, after which Jim isolates himself in the bows of the lifeboat.

The following day, and after they have all seen the last lights of the *Patna* going down into the ocean, the castaways are picked up by a cargo ship that is heading in the opposite direction. They only arrive at their port of destination six days later. The captain hurries to the port authorities to make a declaration of shipwreck. It is at this point that he and his companions learn the truth: the *Patna* did not in fact sink; it was taken in tow by a French gunboat and brought back to port with its pilgrims. So just at the point when the captain is presenting himself as a miraculous survivor of a sudden shipwreck, he finds himself in the ignominious and ridiculous position of having abandoned a ship that has not sunk. The *Patna's* disappearance had in fact lent credibility to the slightly arranged version of the rescue given by the captain and his accomplices, closing the affair in spite of the suspicions still surrounding it.

The second phase thus gives the affair a new twist by revealing *après coup*, retroactively, for the castaways, the hidden truth. While the revelation of the non-sinking of the *Patna* and the pilgrims' survival has the effect of relieving the drama of its *actual* consequences, it accentuates the cowardice of the crew's flight by throwing suspicion even on the assessment of the danger. At the same time as it evokes the virtual consequences of the abandonment of a ship by its captain and crew, the second phase shows, ironically, that the *Patna* got on very well without them. In short, the significance thrown on the episode retrospectively, confers on it a dimension of burlesque farce in which it becomes difficult to tell whether the protagonists appear in a light that is more odious or more ridiculous.

So we now appreciate Jim's situation: in the first phase, he had experience of failure, of making a mistake whose gravity was on the scale of a tragic dilemma: the alternative choice was death, in the passive and anonymous heroism of respect for a norm of conduct; the second phase *reinterprets* this mistake by shifting the accent from guilt onto shame. It is as if the sources of shame were converging and cumulative: the shame of having failed is compounded by the shame of having failed for no reason; the shame of having been mistaken is compounded by the shame of being discovered in this degrading position; the shame of being exposed to the view and judgements of people is compounded by the fact that his mistake was already known before he was aware of it, even before he had spoken about it *perhaps;* and the shame of thinking that it may have been supposed that he was hiding is compounded by the shame of having to show himself in order to show that he was not hiding.

The affect of shame can thus be intensified infinitely, even in the shame of being ashamed, because it is assumes to the highest degree a dimension of 'diffusion' (A. Green). The destiny of this cumulative shame is one of the knots of the plot. While the captain and his accomplices, acting like vulgar rogues, prefer to disappear, Jim chooses to stay to prove (to himself) that he is not afraid of what he has done: at the court inquiry he will be in the role both of witness and accused; he will take part in a reconstitution of the facts while knowing in advance the sanction that awaits him, namely, the withdrawal of his master's certificate. But this choice itself is questionable: should his shame not have led him to "disappear" like a gentleman in order to avoid this public spectacle which would tarnish the honour of sailors?

The hope emerges that the affair will simply 'go away', along with the shame that it entails.

But beyond the inquiry and the judgement, the affair will never end. For Jim, first of all, who will be pursued by rumours of it in the most distant Eastern ports, before he arrives on Patusan; but also, amongst the sailors, between whom it is inevitably discussed—even if they do not know each other—as soon as they hear about it. It continues to function like an endlessly and painfully exciting enigma. This probably explains why Conrad, starting from the narrative cell of an authentic event, could not content himself with the "short tale" initially envisaged, but felt obliged to unfold its episodes in a long "adventurous and meandering novel".

Conrad's art is to manage the time of the narrative in such a way that the tale of the true/false shipwreck of the *Patna* seems to draw endlessly renewed generativity from the *intolerable* nature of its retrospective significance, concerning which I will try to show the part played in it by unconscious fantasy. At the same time, the tale of the affair gradually delivers, here and there, an undeceived wisdom which will be summed up as follows: 'So the poor young man jumped with the others'. The narrative perpetuates a painful tension, an agonizing struggle, constantly revived, between a certain way of 'seeing things as they are', and the requirements of a code of honour, and of the ideal that it upholds, without which 'everything collapses'. The *motive force* of the Ideal, its relation to illusion, and the risk of its *collapse*, constitute the substance of the ethical questioning of the narrator and of the old sailors whom he addresses.

* * *

I would like to emphasize one particular point of the narrative construction, which is not unlike a major issue of concern in the "analytic scene". *Lord Jim* is marked by the division of the narrator's status: the four first chapters, which present the hero and get the story going, until the collision with the wreck, belong to the convention of the omniscient novelist, who is absent from the story. In a very precise manner, they end with the evocation of the court scene, a scene in which a cold reconstitution of the facts is supposed to unfold, leading to the judgement or sanction. But the evocation of this court scene—one that is anticipated but not followed up—seems designed only to introduce Marlow, who becomes the narrator-actor. This is how things unfold: Jim has noticed a man looking at him, without seeming to be fascinated like the others by the *taboo object that he has become, and 'as if he could see somebody past his shoulder'*, that is, behind the mask that the situation imposes on him.

And in chapter five Marlow speaks: 'Oh, yes, I attended the inquiry'. This sudden break with convention quickly fades into the background since it is very clear that at the court inquiry the die are cast in advance: Jim plays the near-ritual role of the scapegoat, and no disclosure is conceivable. His testimony itself is without meaning since any element of subjectivity is excluded from it. Consequently, the setting aside of the court scene makes way for another scene in which Jim will be able to speak to a similar-Other who is ready to listen to him and to discover that 'the facts explain nothing and certainly not what adds a note of malignant horror to their dreadful character'.

The introduction of Marlow coincides, then, with the opening of an intersubjective scene, and the gap between this new scene and the court scene is a measure of what separates the exposition of the facts from their truthful evocation: the meeting with Marlow opens up for Jim the new possibility of re-evaluating the meaning of the events by addressing speech to the other. Its effect of subjectivation will be indubitable but limited. Marlow embodies, then, the inscription of the story within a subjective temporalization, within an indefinitely readjusted memory: the thread of the narrative is now assured by the speech of Marlow, recounting years later, to friends, what had been said between Jim and himself first, and later on, with witnesses. The narrative thus finds its trajectory, its profound dynamism: it will be able to follow, and will even have to follow, numerous detours and winding paths, with temporal scansions marking anticipations and backtrackings. This process—which sometimes seems to forget its purposive idea—makes the reader pass invisibly from the chronology of the events to the uncertain story that is full of what might not have been, before reaching a sense of an internal necessity, the conviction of an ineluctable destiny.

Marlow can only introduce his story by questioning himself as to how he could have come to find himself involved in this affair. He takes his listeners as witnesses to the enigma of the fact that Jim has chosen him as a *confidant*. He pretends to complain about it, but lets us understand that this 'election'—this transference—was not unconnected with what had brought him to the tribunal and drawn him towards Jim: a *paternal* curiosity, the desire to know the facts in detail, as an experienced captain. But Marlow goes further:

> Why I longed to go grubbing into the deplorable details of an occurrence which, after all, concerned me no more than as a member of an obscure body of men held together by a community of inglorious toil and by fidelity to a certain standard of conduct, I can't explain ... Perhaps, unconsciously, I hoped I would find that something, some profound and redeeming cause, some merciful explanation, some convincing shadow of an excuse. I see well enough now that I hoped for the impossible—for the laying of what is the most obstinate ghost of man's creation, of the uneasy doubt uprising like a mist, secret and gnawing like a worm, and more chilling than the certitude of death—the doubt of the sovereign power enthroned in a fixed standard of conduct. It is the hardest thing to stumble against; it is the thing that breeds yelling panics and good little quiet villainies; it's the true shadow of calamity. Did I believe in a miracle? And why did I desire it so ardently? Was it for my own sake that I wished to find some shadow of an excuse for that young fellow whom I had never seen before, but whose appearance alone added a touch of personal concern to the thoughts suggested by the knowledge of his weakness—made it a thing of mystery and terror—like a hint of a destructive fate ready for us all whose youth—in its day—had resembled his youth (*Lord Jim*, 1900, p. 80).

We can see that for Marlow, discovering a cause, finding an explanation, are mixed up with the very possibility of redemption, with mercy, with forgiveness. The conjunction of the causal register and the moral register would bring about this miracle of warding off the fundamental malaise linked to breaking with the established norm. The impossible nature of the situation lies in the fact that the sovereignty conferred on the symbolic code presents itself as the very condition of meaning; and in the fact that the issue here is to give meaning to its absence, to the breach through which doubt creeps in, eats away at, and invades the subject, making him prey to panic and villainy. Marlow clearly emphasizes both his feelings of sympathy for Jim, and the *egoistic* dimension of his need to restore meaning. But is not the comparison with the analytic scene[2] even more clearly compelling when Marlow tells us what he really thinks or feels? He says that, basically, he did not know why Jim had addressed himself to him, nor even if he was playing up to something, and that 'Jim did not know either; for it is my belief that no man ever understands quite his own artful dodges to escape from the grim shadow of self-knowledge' (p. 102). What better way of announcing the fundamental ambiguity of Jim's story, his attraction and his repulsion for subjective truth, the mixture between the need for control and the call of the unknown, of the unrepresented, between the promise of appeasement and the threat 'of the sinister shadow' of his double.

The novel will focus on the restitution of the interminable *cathartic session* of Jim with Marlow, after a meeting placed under the sign of a reactivation of shame: as he was leaving the first session of the court inquiry, Jim took the man aside—the man whose gaze had struck him—who he thought had called him a 'wretched cur'. In fact, the insult had been made by a fellow with whom Marlow had exchanged a few words and who had stumbled over a dog. Marlow, who was at first taken aback, managed to understand the origin of the misunderstanding and to explain to Jim that he was mistaken, pointing at the sitting yellow dog. The catastrophic meaning of his disdain, and the truth of his projective impulse, affected Jim intensely, even though he could not think about them: how could he admit that his *displaced* revolt was indeed that of a cur struggling against the inner temptation of becoming a *toady*? 'There had never been a man so mercilessly shown up by his natural impulse' (p. 97). But as this betrayal cannot be *subjectivized*, the truth remains inscribed in the gaze of the Other. The redness of shame rising to his forehead is inextricably the cause and consequence of what escapes meaning and diffuses into pure, awfully passivating affect:

'I looked at him [Jim]. The red of his fair sunburnt complexion deepened suddenly under the down of his cheeks, invaded his

forehead, spread to the roots of his curly hair. His ears became
intensely crimson, and even the clear blue of his eyes was dark-
ened many shades by the rush of blood to his head. His lips
pouted a little, trembling as though he had been on the point
of bursting into tears. I perceived he was incapable of pro-
nouncing a word from the excess of his humiliation. From disappointment too—who knows? Perhaps he looked forward to
that hammering he was going to give me for rehabilitation, for
appeasement? Who can tell what relief he expected from this
chance for a row? He was naïve enough to expect anything; but
he had given himself away for nothing in this case. He had been
frank with himself—let alone with me' (p. 98).

The *spectacle* of this shame and this vulnerability modify instan-
taneously Marlow's view of Jim. Seeing him wandering along the
quays, he had been struck both by his incredibly healthy look and
by a certain air of 'impudence'.[3] 'I would have trusted the deck to
that youngster on the strength of a single glance, and gone to sleep
with both eyes—and, by Jove! It wouldn't have been safe. There are
depths of horror in that thought. He looked as genuine as a new sov-
ereign, but there was some infernal alloy in his metal. How much?
The least thing—the least drop of something rare and accursed;
the least drop!—but he made you—standing there with his don't-
care-hang air—he made you wonder whether perchance he were
nothing more rare than brass' (p. 76).

Clearly, this question of the pure and the impure is at the heart
of what constitutes Jim's *personage*, and he would not be a Conradian hero if, until the end, the register of a *demonic* seduction, of an
essential deceit, did not remain in a veiled form. But the uprush of
shame seems to erase this danger: unless he enjoys making Jim feel
ashamed, Marlow has no choice but to *exonerate* Jim in order to get
rid of his own embarrassment in the face of the involuntary admission. 'A single word had stripped him of his discretion, of that discretion which is more necessary to the decencies of our inner being
than clothing is to the decorum of our body' (p. 97). Jim's *mistake*
which carries him obscurely towards a man who attracts him, and
whom he attracts, thus has the significance of a denuding; and the
redness of shame, which becomes the redness of modesty, materia-
lizes the bodily dimension of it. Marlow understands retroactively

the defensive significance of Jim's show of 'impudence', analogous to that of a 'cur'. Impudence is a form of modesty: it seizes the passive experience of *seeming*, by exhibiting it actively, in an inverted form. But the transparency of the defensive mechanism betrays its meaning, and so increases the burden of shame, in a vicious circle, with the effect of the *revealed* exhibitionism.

The acme of shame triggers a clash between the two men, which could be described in psychoanalysis as transfero/countertransferential: 'Jim made an inarticulate noise in his throat like a man imperfectly stunned by a blow on the head. It was pitiful' (p. 98).

It is to flee from this pity that Jim turns on his heels and leaves. Marlow catches up with him and the bond between them is fastened, as it were, by two staples:

1. Marlow reproaches him for running away, to which Jim replies 'never'; and as Marlow explains that he had not meant to say that he was running away, Jim reiterates: 'From no man—from not a single man on earth'. Through this new misunderstanding, Jim reveals the intensity of his projective position, which makes him place the danger he is faced with in a man—to whom it is wise not to show one's 'behind'. Marlow comments on this enigmatically: 'I forebore to point out the one obvious exception which would hold good for the bravest of us; I thought he would find out by himself very soon' (p. 98). At the beginning of this sentence, it is difficult not to think of the temptation for Marlow to remind Jim 'stupidly' that he has already fled once; the rest of the sentence might lead one to think that Marlow is alluding, retrospectively, to the feeling that he has already had that 'the bravest of us' could have acted like Jim on the *Patna*: consequently, this access to the universal experience of flight is designated as that which *therapeutically* had to be discovered by Jim himself.

This interpretation of Marlow's sentence is not lacking in depth: it suggests Jim's attachment to his mistake and the work to be accomplished in order to free himself from it. But it does not tally with the temporality of the tale, and, above all, does not take into account the reference to the flight from a man (rather than from the danger of death). Thinking of the 'grim shadow' of self-knowledge, it would be tempting to suppose that Marlow is referring to the flight from oneself, or from the Other within us, the unconscious. But is it not plausible primarily that Marlow-Conrad is condensing involuntarily the flight from man (bearer of the ideal) and the flight towards man?

Marlow's denial ('I did not say that you were running away from me') designates him as the internal father from whose approach Jim flees.

2. The other staple is no less subtle than the one that results from the phallic challenge that fixes Jim in front of Marlow. Marlow expresses, in an 'idiotic mumble', his regret at having been the cause of a misunderstanding and his refusal to leave him under such a false impression. We can see that shame has changed camp in a moment's exchange. Marlow wants to make his listeners believe that 'the power of sentences has nothing to do with their sense or the logic of their construction' (p. 98). We are not surprised, though, that the 'stupidity' of his phrase seduced Jim: does it not signify the reversal whereby Marlow is now the one who is concerned about the impression he is leaving on the reprobate, the outcast? Jim recovered his wits and cut him short 'with courteous placidity that argued an immense power of self-control or else a wonderful elasticity of spirits—'Altogether my mistake.''' The irony of the adjectives indicates that the defensive valency of this restoration strikes Marlow in terms of what it owes to the denial of psychic reality: 'I marvelled greatly at this expression: he might have been alluding to some trifling occurrence. Hadn't he understood its deplorable meaning?' (p. 99). He had almost understood it, but the grim shadow had been revealed and hidden by the red veil of shame. Now, Jim's answer is 'ready': his mistake was excusable because the people in court, by staring at him so stupidly, had made the utterance of the insult entirely plausible.

And Marlow concludes: 'This opened suddenly a new view of him to my wonder'. This new view concerns Jim's modes of *reaction* in which considerable personal resources and the psychic restrictions that they imply are inextricably associated. This alloy leaves Marlow disconcerted, and this feeling will not change. Nonetheless, the two staples function well: the first links the way that Jim faced up, in front of Marlow, to the latter's silent postulate that Jim would discover the universal experience of fear. The second links Marlow's recognition of his involvement in the incident with Jim's recognition of his subjective responsibility. He can then point out to Marlow that he makes a precise distinction between (a) the court scene where he says he can put up with anything, adding, 'and I can do it too'; and (b) the scene of reality, concerning which he says, 'I can't put up with this kind of thing and I don't mean to.'

At this point Marlow invites him to dinner, and it is on the verandah of Malabar House that they converse together all night in a formidable *session*, the narration of which extends for one hundred and twenty-five pages of the book. The preliminary condition for such an exchange was that it involved the presence of two *gentlemen*. This condition alone could confer on the meeting its interest by guaranteeing the subjective consistency of the tragic conflict of which Jim is the representative, after having been at the centre of it. I wanted to reconstitute this meeting in detail because it shows the extraordinary sharpness of Conrad's intuition, a sharpness that underlies the very possibility of a psychoanalytic approach to the character Jim, or rather to the double character of the pair Jim-Marlow.

* * *

Before narrating this meeting, Marlow introduces an apparently marginal character, but one whose figure provides a counterpoint to Jim's.

The man is a young, famous and brilliant captain, a nautical assessor and an assistant to the judge, who came to see Marlow with a proposition concerning Jim, which I will come back to. Marlow draws a striking portrait of Brierly in two pages. It is the portrait of a man reduced to his personage as a hero, and so full of himself that he would be odious were it not for an almost parodic note that rendered him somewhat pitiful. This short portrait ends with the mention in passing that Brierly had committed suicide by leaping from his ship, the day after Jim's trial. The subsequent account of the circumstances of this suicide merely serves to draw out more clearly the fascinating enigma: 'There was some reason ... it wasn't anything that would have disturbed much either of us two ... Ay, ay! Neither you nor I, sir, had ever thought so much of ourselves' (p. 91).

Brierly plays the role, then, of Jim's double, of a Jim who has *realised his heroic ideal*, but who nonetheless has a hidden, and perhaps very small weakness which alters his self-esteem, just as a diamond is irremediably devalued by a tiny defect. Brierly seems to commit suicide in Jim's place, embodying the melancholic solution to a narcissistic wound which leaves the subject with no other solution than that of identifying himself with the implacable demand of the idea, namely, of destroying the lost object-ego.

* * *

As it is impossible to follow the 'verandah scene' step by step, I will just draw out its main themes.

Marlow's narration is first and foremost that of Jim's tale. We can guess that Jim is going to have to 'resuscitate' the traumatic experience. To be *effective*, Marlow's narration will involve the painstaking evocation of the facts and circumstances which he, as an old sailor, is able to identify. Based on this reality and posed as a common reference, the narration gets going and becomes a pathetic quest for expressivity, a frantic drifting narrative in which *cathartic* discharges and efforts at psychic binding alternate: we know what the *paroxysmal* art of Conrad is capable of.

It is interesting to note that at an initial level, the spontaneity of speech and the effort of representation suffice to induce in Jim a combination of contradictory motives; and by taking Marlow as a witness and making him the guardian of a spoken truth, he initiates a dynamic that will determine how his story unfolds.

Jim's first intention is to make Marlow 'admit' that his evaluation of the state of the bulkhead was judicious, that panic was not an influencing factor. The fact that the ship did not founder must be considered as a *miracle* in the form of the unforeseen resistance of 'these old rusted sheets of iron'. This first *argument* governs, paradoxically, the second: Jim needed to convince Marlow that his decision to stay on board was not an invention after the event: it was an entirely personal decision stemming from a shared ideal. It was thus all the more noble for being lucid with regard to the choice of death that it implied. These two points determine the *heart* of his story, his obsessive motive to emphasize the radical difference between him and the others (the captain and his accomplices). This difference was never abolished—the leap only lasted an instant—and was confirmed by his isolation at the front of the lifeboat. Jim does not deny his mistake: his presence at the inquiry proves it; but he only recognizes his guilt provided that it does not disqualify this subjective difference, and his *capital* in idealism. He *insists* that Marlow recognize that his conscience is against him, which is a way of affirming the superiority of his internal inquiry.

This *clear* demonstration—which appears to be the very cry of truth—nonetheless rests on a blind point: to assert his difference, Jim finds himself bound to the opacity of his jump, to a register of acting out which can only correspond to a psychic hole. However, the work of representation which is based on this obstacle of a radical difference—and of a *local* denial of psychic reality—will call them into question to some extent and relativize them, somewhat advantageously for Jim. How does the *logical* constraint of this very relative integration work? It is striking to note that it results partly from the effects of the non-sinking of the *Patna*, but without being associated for Jim with a sense of relief about the survival of the pilgrims. The so obviously pernicious effect of *après-coup* thus reveals its positive aspect: by requiring the meticulous reconstitution of the facts, the fact that the *Patna* did not sink renders the horror of the situation more concrete and representable. This shared horror in turn emphasizes the radically useless character of a purely sacrificial heroism, and makes the leap into the lifeboat more acceptable. Thus the *representational* struggle against the ignominious shame that sets in after the event displaces the emphasis towards a less infamous mistake, towards a more sharable guilt.

But the operation of *après-coup* brings into play another factor: the miraculous non-sinking of the *Patna* reveals to Jim that he missed the opportunity—also miraculous—of fulfilling the heroic fantasy which had inhabited him since his adolescent dreams. Only a few seconds later and it would have been too late to 'jump'; Jim would then have been the sole master on board, taking the place of the defaulting captain and acceding to the glorious legend which the affair of the Patna would have become for him. It is obviously not possible for Jim to think about the coincidence between his weakness and the grandiose opportunity, and so to become aware of its subjective implications. On the contrary, he explains to Marlow that he had been preparing himself for a long time for such an exploit, but in this case it was far too unforeseeable. Marlow thinks to himself that it is never foreseeable but, in addition, Jim's affirmation is factually inexact as can be seen from the conditions under which he embarked on the *Patna*. Finally, the fact that the Patna did not sink also allows him to objectify his difference: by presenting himself to the court, Jim includes in his acts that which distinguishes him from the vanished captain. The scene of the court inquiry guarantees the *value* of the ethical conflict which underlies the identificatory encounter with Marlow.

Thus, the second phase of the trauma, which first appears as the 'height' of an operation of muzzling owing to shame, also proves to be *fruitful*. It obliges Jim, after the court inquiry, to open himself up to an encounter which makes him (re)discover the use of speech and the desire to speak. This is why, gradually, confident in Marlow's listening, Jim leaves the terrain of proof, of justification, to express the incredible, the burlesque, the paradoxical aspect of the adventure. And this speech, through the connections that it evokes, through the identifications that it mobilizes, weaves some links between the Jim who wanted to stay—or should have stayed—on board, and the Jim who jumped. The exchange with Marlow gradually reveals what is deeply at stake: as soon as the authenticity of his death wish is recognized—a spoken suicide in place of Brierly's mute suicide—Jim can admit to his desire to live.

All the details count, with their incredible vividness, in this 'progression'. One only has to think of the scene on the poop deck where Jim has taken everything in without even looking: a grotesque scene in which the captain and the three others, in their frenetic haste, aggravated by an approaching squall, are struggling to get the lifeboat into the water and arguing furiously. One of the stooges asks Jim for help and faced with his scornful silence calls him a 'coward' because he seems not to want to save his own life. He thus regards Jim as being prey to a bad, false sense of shame linked to wanting to live.

There is also the issue of mistaken identity: Jim substitutes himself for George, whose enigmatic corpse is found on the deck of the *Patna*. This error leads 'the others' to believe that it is indeed George who is there, and then, that Jim has killed George in order to jump in his place. A long murderous confrontation follows in the boat, where the rage against them and the reflex of self-preservation *deflected* Jim's self-hatred towards the outside, just saving him from suicide. One also thinks of the ignoble *overtures* of reconciliation proffered by the captain to ensure Jim's complicity: at the same time as he denounces this move, is he not being ironic in noting that, from their point of view, he was one of them because he had jumped? And was their version not just as true as his own, given that the Patna, as they all believed, had sunk? The reconciliation with the captain is correlative, for Jim, with the moment when he comes closest to recognizing, and making others recognize, that the affair was too much for him, and perhaps for anyone, in such circumstances.

By being as they were, and by acting as they did, the 'others' left him too alone in the face of such an ordeal: the reversal is clear in relation to the heroic theme where it is precisely his difference, his solitude that underlie the exploit. By 'accusing' the captain (and the 'brothers'), Jim adopts the projective register; he recognizes the necessity of an *active seduction*, of his dependency on an identificatory support, a paternal model and/or sibling solidarity.

Jim's tale comes to its climax and conclusion with the mention of the wish to commit suicide which was tormenting him: we have seen the circumstances that made the suicidal tendency less impulsive than the jump into the boat. All night, though, he was tempted to let himself slip into the water; and all day he stayed facing the burning sun, without a hat, as in a medieval ordeal. It was when the captain growled 'You will die' (from the sun) that Jim felt that he no longer wanted to die. But the most convincing detail for Marlow of the truthfulness of the suicidal temptation is undoubtedly the fact that Jim tells him that he had wanted to swim to the place where the ship had foundered to die with the pilgrims.

The very strangeness of the movement, its symbolic sense, is enough to convince Marlow that Jim had had 'a close brush with death'. His presence thus has something as *miraculous* about it as the non-sinking of the Patna, as the survival of the pilgrims sustained by their faith. Jim needs to be considered as a *survivor*, whose near-death alone can wash away the shame. The restoration of his narcissism *hangs closely* on the truth of this death wish authenticated by Marlow. Just when Marlow assures him that he believes in it, he says, 'a mysterious light seemed to show me … the youth within him' (p. 137). Jim is then able to say how he had rediscovered the desire to live, the right to his own existence: if he had stayed on board the Patna, and if the Patna had sunk, he says he would have clung to the slightest spar, to the slightest hope; he would have swum until his strength was exhausted in the hope of being rescued. This deferred self-revelation by Jim, as we can see, illustrates well his *fascination* by the deadly heroism of shipwreck, by the idea of 'going down with it'. The culminating point of his narration, extending the psychic work begun in the boat, is this reconciliation with the desire to live. So there is no shame in wanting to live? This is the question that Jim's journey raises as it comes to and end. Jim eventually gets to the point of recognizing the universal character of fear.

And yet, to explain his presence in court, he says: 'I am a gentleman: I wasn't going to be frightened of what I had done' (p. 139). This is a very ambiguous statement because naturally, a gentlemen should not be afraid of answering for his actions; but, on the other hand, Jim also seems to be saying that finally there was no shame in being afraid. But the problem Jim is faced with, precisely, is that of the relation between the initial denial of fear and what he did; so much so that his statement indicates, in the form of negation, that in admitting the possible existence of fear, he might begin to be afraid of what it could make him do. Jim seems to evince the permanent confusion in him between the experience of fear and acting out.

It seems here that for him, overcoming the fear of facing the court inquiry might function as a retroactive annulment of the fear whose consequence is at the origin of his appearance in court. Jim hopes for a sanction which will close the affair, in the sense of a psychic *muzzling*.

* * *

Conrad centres the entire end of the encounter between Jim and Marlow on the ambiguity of this 'need for punishment'. Marlow manifests a movement—which may be qualified as 'countertransferential' which is the echo of, the return to a first phase to which I referred earlier, in which Brierly came to propose him something. Brierly's scornful air of boredom at the inquiry in fact hid a feeling of anxious irritation: 'Why are we tormenting that young chap? He asked Marlow, who replied, 'Hanged if I know, unless it be that he lets you' (p. 91). Marlow is thus, a priori, perplexed by what is driving Jim to be there: a certain courage perhaps, to which Brierly retorts that it was more a case of cowardice; Brierly expresses his exasperation: Jim is done for in any case; and the conduct of a gentleman would have been to disappear instead of permitting this abominable exhibition to take place, bringing shame on the seamen's profession as a whole and on their confidence. Marlow points out that it costs some money to run away, to which Brierly replies, 'Does it? Not always' (allusion to suicide); and he proposes to give Marlow some money to give to Jim to help him 'clear out'. Marlow refuses energetically, mainly because he needs to oppose Brierly's arrogance. So for Brierly, the really courageous thing to do for a gentleman, would have been to disappear, eventually 'twenty feet underground'.

The second phase is marked by a surprising resumption of this theme by Marlow. In relating it, he does not hide from his listeners that he is the one who is in question. Just when his very *extreme* exchange with Jim ends, late in the night, he offers him some money to clear out, as Brierly had suggested. It is an *immoral* proposition, completely absurd and out of place, and obviously doomed to failure.[4]

This proposition is at odds with Marlow's general line of conduct, having up till now played the role of an attentive and reserved listener. How does Marlow account for his impulsive act? His indications are fragmentary but profound. Jim's narration has made him share the suffering endured, in particular at the inquiry, and, suddenly, he can no longer tolerate the idea of Jim exposing himself to the last hearing. 'It is heartrending enough as it as', and he hopes to spare him 'the mere detail of a formal execution' (p. 154). This movement of compassion is strong enough to make him irritated by Jim's refusal and switch into a ferocious attack: he tells Jim brutally: 'I confess I am totally unable to imagine what advantage you can expect from this licking of the dregs' and feeling enraged, adds, 'I am dashed if I do'. It is not difficult to imagine the reaction of Jim who is taken aback and disappointed: 'I've been trying to tell you all there is in it ... But after all it is *my* trouble' (p. 156). Jim's reaction arouses in Marlow the sense of having lost all confidence in himself, at the very moment when Jim seems to have given up on him as an interlocutor. Jim then mumbles between his teeth: 'Not one of them would face it ... I won't shirk any of it.' How should Marlow's impulse, under the aegis of compassion, be *interpreted*? Marlow was well placed, was he not, to see the necessity for Jim to see the process through to its end? It seems that his *acting* is connected with the approaching natural end of their dialogue and to the sense of unease that it arouses.

Marlow seems to want to *do more* for Jim, and to do this he must return to the terrain of events and actions; in so doing, he disqualifies the symbolic register of their exchange, and seems tempted to disown it. Concretely, he shatters the transference and breaks off his relations with Jim: he finds himself in the same position as Brierly who wanted to get Jim to clear out.

Marlow's compassion is thus deeply ambivalent. This heartrending story has no doubt been terribly shaking and exciting, and has drawn him closer to Jim: is it not true that he feels ashamed about the pleasure he derives from it? does he not have the impression he has taken the place of the *tormenting* judge, and is he not tempted, as a result, to pronounce an acquittal in the form of a nullification (echoing, in short, a certain logic of Jim's)? So the remark, 'it's gone on long enough' not only concerns the court scene, but the very scene of their exchange.

Marlow's deep ambivalence is confirmed by another indication. He recognizes, within himself—like Brierly—that Jim is 'guilty and done for' (p. 154). Now this observation occurs just when, in the middle of their dialogue, Jim regains hope: 'he believed where I had already ceased to doubt. There was something fine in the wildness of his unexpressed, hardly formulated hope' (p. 155). This hope irritates Marlow and his sense of reality: does it not reflect Jim's words, 'I know, but all the same', the denial out of which the mirage of another 'opportunity' flowers? No doubt his experience as a mature man makes him fear new wounds for Jim and refuse the limits of his own power. But Jim's faith also reminds him that he is beyond the age when hope sustains life: hence the emergence of a ferocious wish to 'disillusion' Jim, in the manner of one who 'only sees things as they are'.

The crucial point is that Marlow challenges Jim's *desire* concerning the court inquiry: he denounces the close link in Jim's mind between this hope and the benefit, the advantage to be derived from the passing of judgement. Without any doubt, he sees in it the infantile illusion according to which the parental sanction is equivalent to forgiveness and effaces the wrongdoing, in which the egocentric sense of being 'on the straight and narrow'—judged and sanctioned—substitutes itself regressively for the necessity of taking into account 'simple and hard reality'. Even more crucially, I think, Marlow manifests repugnance towards the eroticization of public humiliation, towards Jim's masochistic exhibitionism, towards anti-traumatic hysterization.

Is this not precisely what has just happened between them? We can only understand the enormity of Marlow's blunder by postulating an acute sense of unease concerning the pleasure/suffering arising from and during their exchange: hence the displacement on to the scene of the inquiry, a displacement loaded with all the contradictions that I have just mentioned. Their 'communion in the night' thus culminates in a formal 'execution'.

It is only after this last hearing and Jim's conviction that Marlow finds his true place once again. He now helps Jim (who is badly cut up) by offering him a place (his own hotel room) and a long period of silent presence (he deals with his mail). He then gives him a letter of recommendation for a distant friend: help which is undoubtedly *material*, but symbolically significant owing to the confidence he places in Jim by putting his own reputation on the line for him.

If I have emphasized Marlow's *countertransference*, it is because it bespeaks of the depth with which Conrad recreates, thanks to the illumination provided by the exchanges between them, the profound ambiguity of Jim's 'solution', and consequently the ambiguity of the answer to the problem posed by Jim. Marlow's hesitation is identifiable right up to his last confidence concerning Jim: 'if he had not enlisted my sympathies, he had done better for himself—he had gone to the very fount and origin of that sentiment, he had reached the secret sensibility of my egoism' (p. 155). A statement, in short, that is no more enigmatic than the phenomena it is concerned with. The source, the origin of the sympathy? *Einfühlung*, or empathy, Freud would say, referring to the most primitive forms of identification. Marlow shows clearly that this identification is ambivalent. It is not only comprised of sympathy because Jim 'had done better for himself', i.e., he had gained a certain ascendancy over Marlow. Marlow clearly suggests that this identification is a 'voluntary constraint' which both satisfies and menaces his egoism, even though he is not sure whether he derives pleasure from it or suffers from it more. In fact, he has not left off wondering, from the very beginning, what drove him to become Jim's confident.

So Marlow does not remain a simple, pure narrator. He indicates clearly that Jim resembles both the son that he would have liked—and feared—to have and the young man that he once was. His blunder makes him change places, and this change reflects the instability of Jim's symbolic references. During the night, Marlow adopts an oblique position in relation to the inquiry, that of a distanced paternal function. He assumes a *maternal* position in which compassion reveals the desire for omnipotence: he adopts the position of depriving/protecting Jim from the judicial body and its sanction. But this change reflects his changing view of the inquiry which becomes the locus of a perverse ritual in which the tormenting father satisfies the masochistic child. Marlow is now the one who wants to stop Jim from making a shamefully enjoyable 'exhibition' of himself.

By trying to make Jim his 'creature', by wanting to lose him in order to save him, by arranging a disappearance/reappearance equivalent to death and resurrection, Marlow acts out a parental fantasy in which the paternal/maternal duality proves precarious and uncertain. Beyond the register of phallic control and complicity between sailors through which Jim can repair his wounded narcissism, this countertransferential fantasy contains the mark of Jim's identificatory confusions.

More immediately, the transition from the Marlow who is seduced by the grandiosely cursed Jim to the Marlow who acts to 'save' Jim necessarily corresponds to a virtually present reversal in Jim, i.e., of no longer being an active subject exhibiting himself, but an object passively manipulated, who lets himself down.

* * *

This recapitulation of the themes of the novel has shown us the intrinsic dynamic at work in the ordering of representations through the process of narration into ordered representations. However, the necessary division of the scene of 'reconstitution'—between the court and the verandah of the hotel Malabar—is partly reproduced within the encounter between Jim and Marlow. The scene between Jim and Marlow is comparable to the analytic scene inasmuch as it is entirely organized in terms of the effects of the transference and countertransference, that is, of the acted reactualization through speech and acts of the traumatic event. Jim first calls on Marlow to act as a witness to the fatal chain of circumstances, to the fundamentally passivating dimension of the tragic situation that he had to *suffer*; but what he says changes register as the narration of the scene organizes a narrative scene: the narrating of the action turns into the action of the narrative in which Jim appears as the subject. By making Marlow experience what he has suffered, and through the reciprocal identification between them, he begins to re-inscribe the adventure in terms of what is representable and thinkable. The work of linking between word- and thing-presentations fills the psychic void of shame. Basically, through the multiplicity of the themes, the deployment and linking up of their contradictions, the essential drift of this narrative, the vocation of this speech, is to make 'dishonour' thinkable and to give shame the status of an inescapable affect.

At the end of his narration, the question as to why Jim jumped is not more pressing than that of knowing why he would not have jumped. The enigma is now focused on the way that he 'jumped': does its character of *acting*, of being subjectively 'outside-meaning', owe something to his denial of being attached to life, to his refusal to admit the slightest trace of terror in him? Conrad has already told us what is essential about this at the beginning of the novel, and in just a few words. I will come back to this.

Before doing so though, I would like to emphasize how Conrad's writing illustrates certain crucial issues in Freudian metapsychology. Conrad's art allows him to play with the evocative power of words and to confer on the visual representations that they evoke a hallucinatory intensity evoking the Freudian conception of the significance of the first psychical act. There are moments when all distance seems to be abolished between words and things, when words are imprinted on the psychic surface in 'letters of fire', or, on the contrary, vanish into thin air to the point of becoming indistinguishable from 'visions'. These *hallucinated* moments seem to satisfy, to saturate the need for representation by suppressing the lack which inhabits every representation, and to rediscover a *primitive* satisfaction. These moments nonetheless leave the reader with a sense of dazed incredulity, the impression of a 'scorched' psychic surface. Conrad seems to be aware of this when he inserts these moments within long digressions which allow for a period of recuperation and serve as *preliminaries*. The writer thereby immediately renders tangible a fundamental Freudian question: what is it that pushes Jim to want to repeat the abominably painful and heartrending experience that he has been through? Is the compulsion to repeat in the service of the pleasure principle or is it working beyond it towards a primordial binding? The writing enacts the ambiguity itself of the revival of this traumatic reality, of the penetration of the *overwhelmed* psychical apparatus; it induces in the reader a sort of hesitation: is it a question of bringing into psychic reality what has not yet found its place and meaning, or of effacing it as if nothing had existed? The intensity of what has been seen seems to eventuate in the unreality of a dream, or of a nightmare that is *effaced* on awakening. Conrad defies the limits of what is representable for the reader. The uncertainty about Jim's pleasure/suffering throws light on Marlow's blunder: as long as he experiences Jim's narration as a desperate, forced attempt to bind the traumatic episode retrospectively, his listening is 'innocent' and welcoming. Once the threshold of seduction has been crossed, the excitement of pleasure has welled up, shame and guilt are reactualized in the relationship.[5]

This oscillation between attraction and repulsion for Jim and what he represents contributes to the reader's painful pleasure. The incandescent moments of identification with Jim are almost intolerable and allow the reader to appreciate Marlow's long digressions, which, in turn, just when they could become wearying, turn out to have paved the way for Jim's 'return'. The affair of the *Patna* indeed seems to contain a core of traumatic excitement, which explains why the reader tends to forget the unforgettable *Lord Jim*, just as Marlow wants to make Jim vanish, before he reappears refracted by a whole range of witnesses.

I have emphasized what Marlow's final proposition owed to an unconscious disgust for the virtual masochistic aspects involved in the execution at the court; however, it is no less true that he and Brierly were not wrong in considering that Jim's appearance risked compromising the function of the ideal in those who command ships: after all, the passengers would certainly not be reassured by the idea that their captains are inhabited by heroic fantasies.

* * *

It is time now to examine the meaning of the indications that Conrad gives us about how the affair of the *Patna* becomes part of Jim's history. Two preliminary remarks are necessary, though, to explain the reasons for my approach:

1. Owing to its structure in two phases, the affair of the *Patna* contains within itself its own transposition into a *psychic* reality which is marked—as so often in Conrad's work—by uncanniness.

In fact, the second phase brings back into play, back 'into history', what was definitive and closed in the first phase with its tragic dilemma. The first phase proves retroactively to have only been a menace, whose real consequences shift the accent from a ship-wreck to the shipwreck of honour: psychic activity, at first, par-alyzed, is unleashed in order to 'remake history' with 'ifs'. The second phase opens up, then, a field of eventualities, and reveals an imaginary dimension (within the novel itself). By rendering the first phase unreal, the second phase conjures up the scene of fantasy. In return, the first phase contaminates the second by giv-ing it a sort of mischievous intentionality, by conferring on the double blow dealt by fate the appearance of a personal, malefic destiny.

2. The transformation of the event and its *malign* ingenuousness into a figure of destiny does indeed suggest an effect of the compulsion to repeat and the action of an unconscious determination. Now Conrad has indicated this from the beginning of the book, but he has done so with casual discretion, with an economy such that the reader, if he is *informed,* easily fails to recognize it, like Jim himself, of course. It is Conrad's process of writing alone which must accomplish the invisible osmosis between the historical event with all its uncertain aspects and the dimension of what has *already been played out,* which results from unconscious determination. Only a new operation of *après-coup,* i.e., an oriented re-reading, allows the reader to realize—as Jim does perhaps obscurely—that 'he had always known' that things would turn out like that, because, as Conrad writes, everyone's destiny is inscribed in stone.

3. Conrad says in two pages everything that is to be known about Jim's family situation and the nature of his vacation.

Jim originally came from a parsonage like 'many commanders of fine merchant-ships' (p. 46). The living had belonged to the fam-ily for generations: Conrad evokes the enchanting setting in which the church and its parsonage are situated. But Jim has four brothers and 'when after a course of light holiday literature his vocation for the sea had declared itself he was sent at once to a training ship for officers of the mercantile marine' (p. 47). Each word has its weight in these elliptical formulations which I must comment on with a view to making an interpretive construction.

Jim's vocation for the sea is based only on reading, on the imaginary realm. The attraction for the sea relates only to the difficulty of separating internally from the mother. One can imagine what a forced separation represented for Jim, a decision that takes the reader's fantasies literally. Conrad is careful to reveal the nature of Jim's heroic fantasies: 'He saw himself saving people from sinking ships, cutting away masts in a hurricane, swimming though a surf with a line; or as a lonely castaway, barefooted and half naked, walking on uncovered reefs in search of shellfish to stave off starvation. He confronted savages on tropical shores, quelled mutinies on the high seas, and in a small open boat upon the ocean kept up the hearts of despairing men—always an example of devotion to duty, and as unflinching as a hero in a book' (p. 47). Conrad details here a veritable catalogue of *typical* childhood fantasies. These fantasies correspond, according to Freud, to an unconscious oedipal wish of heroically seducing the maternal object by one's phallic power. As for 'saving' from drowning, it has the meaning of a birth: bringing people back to life by getting them out of the water.

The nature of these fantasies in no way prejudges the possibility of their subsequently being transformed into a sublimatory wish and a sustaining Ideal. However, Conrad clearly indicates the failure of this transformation in the collective life of the training ship. But was not this failure already inscribed in the circumstances of the departure?

How can one not accord all the importance it deserves to Conrad's allusion to the father's utilization of Jim's 'vocation' to resolve conveniently a future problem of inheritance? Was the father's haste in 'sending him away' not a sign of a sort of paternal spinelessness? Conrad proposes just one ironic comment on the parson: 'he possessed such certain knowledge of the Unknowable as made for the righteousness of people in cottages without disturbing the ease of mind of those whom an unerring Providence enables to live in mansions' (p. 46). It is clear that the father's ideal is more a matter of ease of mind than of virtue and that the 'arrangement' with Providence which seals Jim's expedition is indeed one that contributes to making it Unknowable; but also one that undermines an ideal and makes a subject fallible, without his realizing it.

Conrad is also very brief on Jim's 'training'; he is just described as a strong and talented lad who gets by 'quite well'. However, 'his station was in the fore-top, and often from there he looked down, with the contempt of a man destined to shine in the midst of dangers ...' (p. 47). So Jim does not see himself as being in a situation of identificatory rivalry with his peers, but is possessed by an attitude of loftiness which excludes him.

Conrad nonetheless describes in great detail an anecdote which has all the significance of a screen-memory: it is the 'first' opportunity which presents itself of saving someone, during a sudden gale on the Thames. Jim is on his bunk (is he sleeping? or fantasizing?) when there is a call: 'Something's up. Come along'. Once on deck, Jim is caught in the unfurling of the elements: 'There was a fierce purpose in the gale, a furious earnestness in the screech of the wind, in the brutal tumult of earth and sky, that seemed directed at him, and made him hold his breath in awe. He stood still' (p. 48).

This moment of terror prevents him from taking part in the rescue of some men who have fallen off another boat into the water. A lifeboat is lowered into the water, but has difficulty in getting clear of the training-ship: Mr Symons, who was directing the manoeuvre yelled out to the young sailors: 'Keep stroke, you young whelps, if you want to save anybody! Keep stroke!', and the boat got clear. At this point, Jim, who had pulled himself together, wanted to jump overboard. But he 'felt his shoulder gripped firmly: "Too late, youngster."' The captain of the ship laid a restraining hand on the boy and Jim looked up towards him with the pain of conscious defeat in his eyes. The captain smiled sympathetically: 'Better luck next time. This will teach you to be smart' (p. 49).

There is something fascinating in noting that the scene of the *Patna* reproduces this one, with a series of inversions which play on the meaning of 'saving and jumping'. Here, the lifeboat, in order to save people, takes the risk of moving away from the ship; on the *Patna*, the cutter, (at first it is stuck on board) gets clear of the ship and saves its occupants, while condemning the ship's passengers to death; here it is too late for Jim to jump because he experiences a moment of terror; on the *Patna*, he jumps out of terror; here the good captain restrains him, while on the *Patna*, the bad captain induces him to jump. Here, he wants to jump, but it is too late for the exploit; on the *Patna*, *he jumps too soon (albeit at the last moment)* and misses the opportunity of covering himself in glory. In both cases, he seems obliged to stick close to the captain.

Conrad describes very precisely the frankly *pathological* manner in which Jim reacts to the incident.

After the triumphal return of the cutter—which brought back two men—the tumult of wind and sea, which had triggered his *persecutory* anxiety, very soon seemed contemptible to him, which initially increases his sorrow at having let himself be terrorised by 'vain threats'. But 'now he knew what to think of it ... He could affront greater perils. He would do so—better than anybody.' Not a particle of fear was left' (p. 49).

Conrad assesses well the influence of the shadow cast by a narcissistic exigency taking the form of knowledge about what one must think, of omnipotent control over/by thought processes. How can one better evoke a projective logic which implies the denial of a major part of psychic reality? And how can one fail to be struck by Conrad's piercing intuition when he recognizes the 'mysterious' dimension of terror before the tumult of earth and sky, which he announces with the words, 'Something's up. Come along'—words that are very closely associated for the analyst with the aura of the 'primal scene'. It can be argued, then, that the dangerous nocturnal attraction corresponds to the instinctual irruption which makes the external scene of parental coupling and the internal scene of an uncontrollable, unrepresentable excitement indistinguishable. Jim's projective position means that the anxieties linked to his erotic/heroic fantasies are 'welded' to the external reality of the gale. Jim finds the tumult and menace of wind and sea 'contemptible', a qualifier which eminently concerns 'shameful' parental sexuality. One can see the existence of a paradox in Jim because, although his vocation as a sailor implies confronting the natural elements, respecting the reality of their greatness, their beauty and their menace, he claims to treat them with contempt. The rest of the episode, as Conrad describes it, confirms the subjective impasse in which Jim finds himself: 'Nevertheless, he brooded apart that evening' (p. 49). In order to efface his secret rage and shame, Jim is obliged to resort to envious denigration of what his fellow sailors have achieved, in particular the hero, with the help of the bowman of the cutter. Jim thought this account of heroic deeds 'a pitiful display of vanity. The gale had ministered to a heroism as spurious as its own pretence of terror.' Jim's attempt to detach himself leads him to the edge of a state of derealization with regard to himself and others. 'He felt angry with the brutal tumult of earth and sky for taking him unawares and checking unfairly a generous readiness for narrow escapes', an almost delirious reversal, necessary for the salvation of a grandiose ego. And Conrad adds: 'Otherwise he was rather glad he had not gone into the cutter, since a lower achievement had served the turn. He had enlarged his knowledge more than those who had done the work'. This gives a good idea of the scale of the 'damage' of the 'rationalizing' process, confirmed by the words, 'When all men flinched, then—he felt sure—he alone would know how to deal with the spurious menace of wind and seas.' Jim's subsequent revenge on the *Patna*—but with a calm sea without wind!—is inscribed under the sign of an Ideal of being 'all alone': but, as such, it resides less in the courage of facing out dangers than in secret, magic knowledge about the 'trickery' involved in danger.

Conrad's conclusion highlights the fragile nature of this narcissistic 'rescue operation': 'the final effect of a staggering event was that, unnoticed and apart from the noisy crowd of boys, he exulted with fresh certitude in his avidity for adventure, and in a sense of many-sided courage' (p. 50).

One might as well say that in the absence of access, even partial, to his psychic reality, Jim is rooted to the compulsion to repeat: the affair of the *Patna* will answer *viciously* the questions that have been evaded.

Between the two, Conrad gives a few indications concerning Jim's career and describes an evolution which gives its full meaning to his presence on the *Patna*.

Jim had been at sea for several years and had become the chief mate of a fine ship. But he had never been tested by those events of the sea that 'show in the light of day the inner worth of a man, the edge of his temper, and the fibre of his stuff that reveal the quality of his resistance and the secret truth of his pretences, not only to others but also to himself' (p. 50).

Nonetheless, destiny arranged things so that Jim's ship would encounter such a drama: but Jim was injured by a falling spar, and lay immobilised in his cabin when the first breeze began to blow, 'secretly glad he had not to go on deck'. But now and again an uncontrollable rush of anguish would grip him bodily, make him gasp and writhe under the blankets, and then the unintelligent brutality of an existence liable to the agony of such sensations filled him with a despairing desire to escape at any cost. Then fine weather returned, and he thought no more about it' (p. 50).

In the context of a regression permitted by this injury, Jim, deprived of any capacity for action, was very close to recognizing the lure of his vocation. Conrad had already indicated, moreover, that the only real reward of the sailor, 'the perfect love of the work', was a notion that eluded Jim. What follows shows this in a veiled form: Jim finds himself convalescing in a hospital in an Eastern port, and discovers the sweetness of the East. He also discovers that there are only two kinds of sailors: the adventurers who have preserved their energy and live ahead of civilization in the dark places of the sea; and the others, serving as officers on country ships and who 'were attuned to the eternal peace of eastern sky and sea'. They are waiting for a stroke of luck. 'In all they said—in their actions, in their looks, in their persons—could be detected the soft spot, the place of decay, the determination to lounge safely through existence' (p. 52). Jim is fascinated by these men, and alongside original disdain there grew up in him a new sentiment for the art of doing well on such a small allowance of danger and toil.

Would it not be true to say that on the other side of the world Jim has rediscovered the temptation of the family nest, of a passive, protected and almost parasitical situation? Are not these men who are strongly averse to taking risks reminiscent of the hidden side of the father?

Jim could also have stayed in the English navy with its tradition and its training structure. But, giving up the idea of going home to England, he took a berth as chief mate on the *Patna*. If the sailor's destiny is to constantly leave the place of origin and to strive indefinitely to return to it (the Odyssey), Jim's choice clearly shows that in deciding not to return to England, he has found the path of the *origin*: decay and shame are not far away.

By embarking on the *Patna*, he has, as it were, kindled this 'place of decay', he has opened up the soft spot, which makes him similar to the captain, but which had already infiltrated the 'pure metal' of his phallic idea. He has never been less prepared to face difficulty, since he has now become accustomed to the 'eternal peace' of Eastern sky and sea: but even on a calm night, 'something can happen' in the depths. Jim's 'casualness' is inscribed in the facts: the *Patna* is not prepared either, since its boats are insufficient in number and its iron is rusty; Jim was thus the captain's 'accomplice' well before he jumped overboard into the boat.

A very close re-reading of the beginning of the novel shows how the adventure of the *Patna* and Jim's way of being are inextricably linked in the story. It is this link that will be the object of my attempted interpretive construction. The portrait that Conrad paints of the young Jim is so precise and so deep that it could illustrate a certain psychopathology of adolescence, in particular concerning the difficulties of the Superego organization and of the function of the Ideal at this period. I would just like to point out that, from the metapsychological standpoint, the structuring of a Superego which acts as a guarantor for the consistency of the Ego ideal depends on a sufficient renunciation of oedipal investments which have become incestuous. It is the desexualization characteristic of a successful identificatory process which allows for the constitution of a sufficiently impersonalized agency. The differentiation between the Ego and the Superego then supports the Ego's task of gaining autonomy, while preserving the gap between the Ego and its Ideal, a gap which preserves the desire and the sublimatory realizations of a stable secondary Narcissism. Conrad's indications concerning Jim's father throw light on the precarious nature of his identification with a paternal figure, the recourse to an infantile register of omnipotence, and a magic incorporation of the seaman's code feeding the denial of reality. I am tempted to add that the absence of any reference to his mother can be interpreted as the negative trace of an unconscious fixation to her. But hasn't Conrad already mentioned Jim's 'seduction' by Eastern sensuality? and the model offered by the men who know how to 'take advantage' of it? The rigidity of Jim's earlier organization scarcely allows for reorganization and compromise and we can sense quite clearly that the voluptuous languor of the East presents itself as a pure alternative to the former heroic ideal. This is why Conrad designates this seduction as a 'place of decay' which threatens Jim's very identity. It corresponds to a global regression in which the emergence of instinctuality signifies an invasion resulting in passivity. Deprived of the prosthesis of the code of the English navy, Jim's ideal could fall apart, and the shaky Superego could regress to its origins in the parents of a primitive scene full of sound and fury.

* * *

Through an identification with Jim that is often as ambivalent as Marlow's, the reader's intuition makes him sense more or less obscurely the circular links between the sudden, opaque nature of his failure in what was undoubtedly a terrifying situation and the excess of his heroic fantasies. There seems to be profound logic connecting his sudden abdication in the face of the nocturnal catastrophe and the fascination that it must have exerted; the expectation—the quest?—of a trauma and the secret incapacity to 'master' it; the phallic posture and the sudden experience of being rendered passive. I want now to try and sift out the foundations of this intuition.

The existential themes which inhabit Conrad and serve as a source of inspiration for his novels have their own coherence and contradictions. But it seems to me that the agonizing depth of his writing resides in the connection of these themes with unconscious life, and in the shame that they express. The episode of the *Patna* is treated by Conrad as an event, in the full sense of the word, with its burden of uncertainties, and with the sequence of unforeseeable circumstances which weave its dramatic plot. And yet, it seems tailor-made to *reveal* Jim's truth: it seems to concern him in the same way that the first storm was directed *against him*. So it is not only that Conrad contrives the margin of freedom so that the ordeal manifests the strength or the weakness of a man; nor can one say that Jim's case 'illustrates' a conflict of a universal nature between self-preservation and honour, between fear and moral prescription. Conrad 'invisibly' turns the encounter between Jim and the *Patna* into the manifestation of an unconscious determination. The deep logic of his art, at the very moment when he is reconstructing faithfully the reality of an extreme situation, is to transfigure it into the unreality, the surrealistic dimension of a nightmare: but a nightmare which is Jim's own personal nightmare, emanating from his dream life, welling up, as if by necessity, from his own psychic organization and its failures. The magic of Conrad's writing—within the novel itself—has the effect that, in the reader's mind, the dilemma of knowing what is real and what is imaginary is suspended. The truth of the narrative is to confer on what 'happens' the weight of a subjective necessity, the sense of destiny. Through its demonic ingenuousness, repetition—in its two phases—dramatizes the effect of an absent Unconscious cause. The burlesque, carnival-like tone of the traumatic scene evokes the uncanniness which, as Freud showed, is linked to the return of the repressed and especially of modes of thinking that 'one thought had been overcome', that is to say, belonging to magical animism. Consequently, Conrad's writing proposes a series of thoughts whose narrative necessity is both evident and enigmatic. By separating them out associatively, I have been able to identify the core fantasy underlying the generativity of the affair of the *Patna*: 'a small boat detaches itself from the big boat: for life or for death?'

* * *

A first approach designates the two-phased scene of the Patna as a double punitive response to Jim's heroic fantasies, and to his recent conversion to the easy way of life. It thus implies two distinct sanctions:

1. The situation of the first phase, which is a tragic reality, seems to be an 'overbid' in relation to the dramatized content of the fantasies. There is a radical contrast between the sense of omnipotence of the author of the fantasies—who is also their hero—and the sense of total helplessness on the *Patna*. The dramatization 'caricatures' the heroic act by rendering it both passive and useless; the code of honour seems only to require resignation to death without glory. Could one not say that it signifies for Jim the necessary limitation of fantasy activity by the paroxysm of a *forced* demonstration?

2. The second phase contrasts with the first just as the moment of awakening follows the nightmare: *it concerns the return to land*. It is inevitable that the non-sinking of the *Patna* means that the first phase has to be reinterpreted, for one thing, as damage, the danger of which is exaggerated by Jim's state of panic. From this point of view, there is a natural connection between Jim's casualness, his embarkation with a spineless captain on a poorly prepared ship, and the incapacity to face up to a delicate situation. There is a direct echo here between Jim's leanings towards Eastern life and the *jump* into the lifeboat.

The contrast between the two phases thus suggests a double register of sanction by 'reality': in phase one, the tragic reality *surpasses* fantasized fiction; in phase two, the reality of the non-sinking and the court inquiry condemns practical irresponsibility. However, as soon as one tries to articulate the two phases, an alternating echoing effect occurs which confuses things. It is tempting to link the contrast between the two phases to the opposition between what is imaginary and what is real, which would assume diverse meanings: between the tragic and the commonplace, and between the illusion of the ideal and the pettiness of daily life; but the opposition is also present in each of the two phases: between the duty of dying and the desire to live first of all, and then between the duty/desire to appear in court and the wish to disappear. The most global effect of the articulation of the two phases is that of seeming to couple glory and death on the one hand and life and shame on the other. But this global effect does not throw light on the dynamics of the echo. It is necessary to try and describe it more closely, to cross the barrier which separates the preconscious themes from the logic of unconscious fantasy.

* * *

Conrad takes great care to preserve the ambiguity which results from the uncertain character of the resistance of the old rusty iron. This ambiguity allows for the commutation between the two *versions* of the affair. In fact, the second phase tempts one to make what could be described as a reassuring interpretation of the episode, an interpretation that is no doubt necessary to lend support to the fictional identification. If phase one sanctioned Jim's imaginary heroism, phase two reveals, retrospectively, that the affair in fact involved no more than a dangerous situation, while sanctioning Jim's incompetence. The moral of the story is that Jim is punished where he sinned: the principle of an 'eye for an eye' requires him to be punished commensurately with his sin of pride, of arrogance. Is not the sanction of the inquiry softer than the supreme punishment? It is normal and even 'normative': it should 'serve as a lesson'.[6]

This interpretation, scarcely tragic and Conradian, seems 'edifying'. But it is interesting to consider its 'infantile' pertinence: it illustrates the logic of the castration complex, which is so uncertain in Jim. The first phase may be said to correspond to the threat of castration, amounting to annihilation; the second phase shows that it was only a threat, but one whose consequences need to be taken into account: giving up oedipal objects, accepting the limits of the gap between the subject and his Ideal. The themes underlying the scene of the *Patna* could, from this perspective, be reduced to an 'if ... then' situation; for example, 'if you abandon yourself to your auto-erotic activities instead of doing your duty as a sailor, you will meet with a situation that is too much for you, and you will find yourself in front of a court, with the risk of being deprived of what allows you to sail.'

This first interpretive approach is hardly convincing; but its implicit, virtual presence sheds light on a certain level of anxiety at which the reader would sometimes like to stop in order to protect his pleasure from an excessively painful participation. But Conrad makes a deeper menace loom on the horizon which challenges Jim's narcissistic identity, stemming precisely from the weakness in his phallic organization. The mode of actualization of the traumatic scene in its two phases conjures up such an intensity of regressive ideas, of archaic anxieties, that the reader is traversed by the depth of the subjective impasse in which Jim finds himself enclosed by the testing of his limits.

In the second phase, in spite of certain elaborative nuances, we notice the absence of a potentially conceivable structuring effect. Jim integrates practically nothing of what the second phase makes of the adventure retroactively: he seems to remain indifferent to the fact that the ship and the pilgrims have been saved, even though it could 'delimit' his guilt; he cannot conceive at all of the possible relation between what has happened and his own 'dispositions'; he says nothing about the unprepared state of the ship and its crew, nor about the fitting out of the ship, which could lead him towards a real and responsible sense of guilt. He seems to remain *fixed* to his fall, and only recalls the second phase insofar as it allows him to establish what differentiates him from the captain and the others, i.e., his voluntary appearance at the court inquiry.

If Jim seems indefinitely preoccupied by the first phase, it is because, in spite of its tragic character, he prefers it because it throws light on his failure and attenuates his intolerable narcissistic wound owing to the imposing nature of the ordeal. If I position myself now solely within the register of psychic reality, the atrocious dilemma seems to me to realize, while simultaneously masking, two desires which are both deeply unconscious and yet almost rendered present by Conrad's writing. The first can be seen in the almost absurd aspect of the seaman's code: would it not be true to say that it seems coloured by a cruelty that is strictly speaking sadistic? Under the

anonymous mask, under the impersonal prescription, is lurking—
according to the logic of masochism qualified by Freud as *moral*—
the figure of the punishing father who sent Jim to the training ship.
The masochistic pleasure dissimulated in the logic of the scene is
one of being loved/hated by the father in the regressive instinctual
mode of sadomasochism. To this may be added the desire to take
vengeance on the father by denouncing at one and the same time his
seduction, his indifference, and his infanticidal wish. It is not only
by jumping that Jim challenges so deeply the norm of conduct! Is it
not fair to describe Jim on the poop deck as one who is crucified for
honour's sake? Who must he join?

The second desire is more manifest but more obscure in its
expectations: the jump into the boat is at once a plunge into the
abyss of shame and a new coming to life. It thus represents a birth,
a delivery, even though these are contaminated by the echoes of a
primal scene that cannot be integrated. In order come to life, Jim
has to tear himself away from the sides of the *Patna*, which is sinking with its pilgrims. In the logic of primary processes, this means
that in order to come to life he allows the *Patna* and its human
cargo to die: it's either him or them.

This murderous act conjures up a double figurative image: on one
level, the *Patna* is the menaced/menacing maternal container from
which one must escape, which one has to get rid of in order to 'sur-
vive'. On another level, the *Patna* is a paternal penis which is going
to sink and lose itself in the mother, owing to a non-identified object,
and because there are too many children on board. It is necessary to
spring from it, fall off it in order to (re)gain firm ground.

This figurative division also applies to the lifeboat, which may be
identified with 'the little thing that can be detached from the body'
(penis, child, faeces); it is the paternal penis withdrawing from the
maternal body to avoid being engulfed (in the first rescue scene
it was what brought the drowned men back on board). It carries
away—unfortunately—some little brothers; Jim is not alone, even
if he isolates himself in the bows. The lifeboat is also Jim himself,
tearing himself away from the code of honour and/or the maternal
body. Finally, the lifeboat is Jim's penis, while Jim is identified with
the *Patna*: the jump, with its spatial hiatus and its temporal caesura,
dramatizes the very horror of castration. I am a little fearful that
my construction may appear *theoretical*: but it springs from Conrad's

hallucinated writing! How can one fail to be struck by the obsessive and misplaced importance that he confers on the difficulty of men to cut the ties between the small boat and the *Patna*? How can one fail to note that it is when Jim refuses its help that he is called a coward because he 'won't save his own life'? How can one fail to see that George, the man who dies from heart failure as a result of his efforts of 'separation', is Jim's double, the corpse that he leaves on the *Patna* before taking his place in the boat?

The jump into the boat is an extraordinary condensed dramatization of the equivalence between birth/separation and castration: more precisely, Jim jumping into the boat is Jim accepting life without 'castration'.

Which shameful desire is hidden behind what renders this scene so intolerable for Jim? It is no doubt linked to the image of the captain: a monstrous image owing to a sort of lack of differentiation arising from obesity and spinelessness. The jump into the boat repeats, in a paroxystic and highly condensed form all the seductions of the 'embarkation' on the *Patna* which then become traumatic and intrusive. It is by no means simple to unravel the different strata without running the risk of seeming to proceed arbitrarily. Yet, several points can be emphasized:

- The captain is first of all the other half of the divided paternal image, the spineless father of all the compromises, of all the *jouissances*. By desiring the castration involved in jumping, Jim melts in his arms, as it were, *pour une petite mort*[7]: does this eclipse not designate a feminine passivation?
- But the captain is equally an undifferentiated paternal/maternal image, a monstrous phallic chimera, both penetrating and penetrated.
- Finally, owing to his elephant-like aspect, he incarnates an animalistic, archaic image, the breast/belly of primitive, cannibalistic orality, an unrestrained, lawless, instinctual greed which is indifferent to the fate of its objects: 'pure' gluttony'. At this level, the jump into the boat metaphorizes the confusion of the identification with the primary object, reunion with the overabundant breast, the blessed passivation of being nourished/carried. This pregenital evocation also conjures up the equivalence between Jim's fall and defecation: anal birth and/or mortal or saving expulsion.

The jump into the boat, which enables Jim to join his captain, thus realizes a sudden, unforeseen toppling over into polymorphous and confused instinctuality. One can understand why, for Jim, affirming his radical difference from the captain, is a vital issue of identity.

The interpretation that I have sketched out here of the first phase of the scene of the *Patna* reveals the unconscious network of fantasy which gives profound support to the horror of the manifest situation. It suggests the agonizing struggle in the subject between two positions of desire which resist any solution of compromise in terms of complementarity:

- Staying on board would combine taking possession of the mother and substitution for the faulty father. But the active desire finds itself turned into a passive situation in which the subject is simultaneously crucified by the father and engulfed by the sea/mother: masochistic pleasure culminates in a deadly double incest.
- Jumping into the boat would be to renounce the heroism of death and to choose actively the eroticism of life. But for Jim, this is equivalent to substituting himself for the lost mother and taking her place with the father, to losing his honour with his virility. More radically still, the choice of life seems to require a radical passivation vis-à-vis the demands of the body, vis-à-vis a primary instinctual 'attack' resulting from the failure of projection. The call from the boat is like a siren's song: a deferred primal seduction that is incompatible with subjective identity.
- It is as if a secret collusion between these two positions—under the sign of passivation—nailed the subject to an endless alternative between a death without glory and a life of shame.

Jim's agonizing struggle is directly connected with the perversion dividing the paternal image. It can be expressed simply like this: the *Patna*, a phallic symbol of the transport of life, is what unites and separates the captain—representing experience, tradition, the moral code—and the sea, an element that is sustaining and nourishing, but also menacing.

For the young Jim, the bond between the captain and his ship is as necessary as that between the ship and the nourishing element: the 'office' of captain can only be transmitted to him in conditions which make possible the mourning, i.e., the symbolic murder, of the father.

Now the first phase of the scene of the Patna *dramatizes* the abdication of the captain-father. Let us transcribe it in the form of an attempted dream wish-fulfilment which ends in a nightmare: 'Jim is on watch on a night so black that the sky cannot be distinguished from the sea, both of which are merged in an eternal calm (antithesis of the sudden awakening by the storm). However, 'something happens'; there is a long drawn-out jolt. It is Jim who rushes forward to see what is happening: the bows are dipping into the sea, there is an imminent risk of being engulfed, the rusty iron bulkhead is bulging like the belly of a pregnant woman. Jim knows 'what it means': he shows disdain for the danger which is only an illusion; he knows that by alerting the captain and his brothers, who are cowards, he will provoke their departure and reveal their cowardice to his mother. He will remain the sole master on board—after God—to save the ship and its pilgrims: dawn will break to his triumph'.

But such a hallucinatory realization is too crude, too 'compromising' for the dreamer's Ego: the degree of anxiety increases. Can the accomplishment of taking possession of the mother be distinguished from drowning? Is it necessary to sink with the ship and to remain eternally at the bottom of the sea with the dead children/pilgrims? Is there not a deadly trap here, set by a code that is all the more deceptive in that it has been seductive, pushing Jim towards heroism? Is this code not the reprisal of the ejected father who comes to punish? This deceived/deceiving father has to be found again at any price: but the repulsive seduction that he exerts by calling Jim to the lifeboat is the very same that made him 'subservient' to Jim's wish to eject him; and if he chooses severity, it will be transformed by instinctuality into a crucifying punishment: Jim will be nailed to the poop deck.

Once the scene of the Patna 'succeeds' in separating the captain from his ship, the symbolic reference of the code is adrift and no mediation can help Jim to preserve his psychic organization and his sublimatory options. The scene marks the disorganization of the pairs active/passive and masculine/feminine, leaving 'on the surface' only a binary opposition of pure reciprocal exclusion: phallic/castrated, in which the phallic is tied to death, and the castrated to the shame of living. Jim is obliged indefinitely to go back over the traces of what cannot really become a jump, an élan, and remains a 'letting himself fall'. He thus commemorates the hiatus of his subjectivity: Jim seems to base his identity on the split between his two 'major' identifications: the active/phallic desire for death echoes the desire for castration.

The indefinite return to the first phase is the return to the virtual, to what has not yet happened, to the narcissistic completeness of non-choice. A major characteristic of the first phase is that Jim is the object of a request, a call: the *Patna* is going to 'need' him—like the pilgrim's baby needs his pilgrim father. The code requires something of him. The others ask him for help; the captain calls to him from the boat; he tries to talk him into confirming his version of events. Passivation does not prevent Jim from feeling, on all sides, required, virtually necessary. The Desire of the Other makes him hold firm.

This aspect of things gives us a better appreciation of what is intolerable in the first phase: the divine surprise of the non-sinking of the *Patna* is for Jim the absolute horror, since it means that his absence did not count, that they got by very well without him, just as during the first storm the rescue operation was carried out without him, and during the second storm the ship pulled through while he was lying in his cabin. The third episode, when they slip away quietly in the night, confirms that he is not indispensable to the march of things. The supreme shame is to realize this. One can understand that Jim chooses the court inquiry: he regains some importance there; one understands above all that he treasures his guilt like the apple of his eye: it gives him the makings of omnipotence again which he needs. The second phase, by showing that nothing has happened, signifies the arrival of 'nothing', the menace of a radical disillusionment, which is why it triggers in Jim the barbaric nostalgia for the first phase, and for its masochistic deflagration.[8]

The second phase thus contains the danger of a melancholic depression, which concerns the very meaning of life. The quasi-suicide on the lifeboat made Jim see the possibility of appropriating his life by destroying it, of giving birth to himself. With the eruption of hate, and the admission of wanting to live, he tasted the instinctual, wild savour of life. But by showing him the nullity of the consequences of his absence, the second phase trips him up. My hypothesis is that this situation preceded the affair of the *Patna*: it stemmed from Jim's decision not to return to England. The affair of the *Patna*, from this point of view, is the dramatization of the unconscious psychic effects of the loss of family ties that is denied. The work of mourning this loss was probably no more possible for Jim at this point than it was at the moment of his sudden departure for the training ship or, perhaps, on the birth of his brothers who dislodged him from the status of child-king. The loss may have been masked by an apparent disinvestment. Jim no doubt felt capable of mastering the separation; no doubt he believed that the attraction of the East would replace the memory of the West. But the hardest thing for him was not to cut himself off from his parents: it was, I think, to accept the idea that the parents might cut themselves off from him for ever. It is quite natural to suppose that Jim was inhabited by the fantasy of a triumphal return: his glory would then have satisfied and/or distressed his parents who had 'banned' him after having cherished him.

Disinvesting this idea meant allowing space for the contrary idea that his parents might cease to wait for him. Would they not transfer on to the brothers the love that they had for him, the demand that they addressed to him? In that case, they would do without him: he would have ceased to exist for them. And the unbearable question for Jim would be this: what am I if they no longer miss me? The scene of the *Patna* presents itself as the paroxystic representation of this question. I have emphasized the role of the perverse division of the paternal image and the dehiscence of its identificatory function. The old, projected attracting ideal, returns here—in the form of reprisal—like a *revenant* to whom Jim owes total allegiance, on pain of betrayal. The initiator to the seductive East becomes a guide of abjection.

The second phase, however, marks a certain subjective recovery on Jim's part, through two mediations which assign him a fairer place: on the bench of the accused where, finally, he has to answer for his acts and especially in front of Marlow who recognizes him as 'one of us' just when he becomes an outcast. This recovery will not go as far, however, as to deliver Jim from his compulsion to regard himself as a rescuer or saviour; he remains subject to the requirement to be necessary for the other. He will be obliged to confer on his heroic redemption, in Patusan, a deadly, sacrificial dimension of idealization.

In the interval, he will 'work off' his shame. Make no mistake about it: in his role of wandering outcast, fleeing the rumour of his error, Jim remains faithful to his character and to his 'vocation'. He refuses to allow his error to be trivialized and thereby protects in his imagination a negative celebrity. In a sense, he conserves, in an 'inverted' form, the fantasy of the glorious return. He is undoubtedly inhabited by the fear that his parents will learn of 'what happened': his reputation, in spite of everything, will have crossed the oceans. We may suppose that his fear conceals the hope that they will thereby be obliged to think about him, once again. Is he not saying to them: 'Look at what you have made of me?' In this case, Jim's shame will rebound on them to the point that they will not cease to carry him within them, painfully. This idea is disavowed, but throws light on the persistent eroticization of his internal shame: the need to hide himself is related to the need to exhibit himself; shame and glory are commutable.

* * *

Jim's excessive shame is related to the refusal of all shame, to the refusal of what arouses our first sensations of shame, retrospectively: shame about owing our life to the copulation of a man and a woman, shame about being born *inter faeces et urinas*; shame about having been cradled, caressed, nourished, changed and for having liked that; shame about accepting, under the threat of castration, oedipal compromises; shame about the subtle transactions between the needs of the body and its erogenous zones and the purification of the ideal.

Jim refuses his instinctual impulses because accepting them would imply acquitting the parents, having complicity in the erotic pleasure that they had in conceiving him. In short, Jim rejects the narcissistic exchange which makes us hold to life; he continues to live as the victim of a degrading, compromising seduction. Not being able to 'come to terms' with this first shame—the simple shame inherent to life—exposes him to experiencing every satisfaction as a passivating, desubjectivizing threat, every seduction as primal; ultimately, as a red influx, an elemental unleashing, which lays him bare.

* * *

Addendum

In the work we have just read, I have confined myself to the episode of the *Patna* because the links between the false shipwreck and the issues at stake in the unconscious fantasy of rescuing are particularly close and well-established. But, in consulting the notes I made, fifteen years ago, on Jim's redemptive adventure in Patusan, I realize that I had always retained the hope of following up my analysis. Through the passionate interest that the conquest and final fall of Lord Jim arouse in the reader, the second part of Conrad's book suggests, with the same tragic depth, the effects of unconscious determinations that I thought I had been able to identify in the first part. But I no longer feel able to explore with the same attention the text of the novel, nor to show how the searing intensity of his writing makes the truth of the Unconscious emerge. In particular, I would have liked to show how Jim, in his new space, is caught in the split between the part of him that wanted to stay on board the ship and the part that jumped into the boat: in Patusan, he cannot get out of the subjective trap stemming from the radical hiatus that he has to maintain between the Jim of the past and the Lord Jim that he becomes. Conrad's fictional power allows him to inscribe this dilemma of identity within the fabric of the narrative. Just to take one example: Joëlle, Jim's companion, and his female double, suffers from an obsessive fear that Jim will go back to Europe, just as his father had gone back, 'as they all do'. Now the only thing that could reassure her that Jim will not return is something that he absolutely cannot tell her. I would also have liked to come back to the question of the letter that Jim receives from his father to which he cannot reply, but in which Conrad finally makes the mother appear, a mother, who, hitherto, has a been so present by her absence; the letter also mentions sisters, even though in the initial presentation he only had brothers. The reappearance of the family in the novel confirms that the nostalgia of the impossible return continues to haunt Jim.

I just want to come back to a strange resemblance which directly links the crucial episode of the confrontation in Patusan with that of the jump into the life boat on the Patna. It will be recalled that the bandits who come to steal the treasure of the tribe are commanded by a diabolical character called Captain Brown, and that they have gone up the river between the sea and Patusan on board a rowing boat. But they find themselves encircled within the fort on a bend in the river, and the boat, which has run aground, is no longer of any use to them. So they are stuck in the fort and 'done for'. Now Brown asks Jim either to kill them or to let them go, but not to let them die of hunger (it's worth noting that the theme of orality is already insistent in the first part). Is it necessary to detail the deep analogies between this situation and that of the *Patna*? From the dialogue that takes place between the 'immaculate' young man completely dressed in white and Brown, the black soul, the essential point is that owing to the forced identificatory tie that is formed between them, Jim cannot resist the temptation to be generous: he organizes the 'rescue', the embarkation in the rowing boat, the provision of supplies, in such a way that the bandits can go down the river back to the sea (... and back to Europe?). But Brown cannot forgive Jim for this generosity which humiliates him, and maliciously suspects the motivation for it: he stops off en route to attack and kill Jim's 'brother', the son of the chief. As a punishment for his imprudent act, Jim, who does not defend himself, is executed by the chief, the father. The reader has the feeling that he thus realizes the old wish for a death which delivers him from 'the shame of living'. Joëlle tells Marlow that Jim preferred death to her, saying to her, 'I should not be worth having if I defended myself'.

The second part of *Lord Jim* not only confirms the depth of the unconscious logics which *act upon* Conrad's hero. How can one fail to be astounded by the fact that Conrad rediscovers—unconsciously, one is bound to think—on the site of Patusan the same spatial configuration which sustained, on the *Patna*, the dramatization of the rescue whose precise links with the unconscious fantasy of birth and death, under the aegis of castration, I have tried to demonstrate. The striking creation of the very complex character of Jim translates, with the mastery of writing that it requires, the profound familiarity, the conflictual proximity between Conrad and him. But at another level, the very exact and precise analogies which appear obsessionally in the most dramatic situations assume the value of pure, opaque signifiers. Conrad's writing, which engraves them in the reader's mind, seems to be plugged in, as it were, to the thing-presentations of the unconscious fantasy; it thus creates bewitching feeling of obeying a necessity which transcends its author.

Notes

1. This text is a modified version of the article on shame published in the Review *Adolescence* in 1993, Paris: Editions G.R.E.U.P.P.
2. It is worth noting the concomitance of the dates: *Lord Jim* was written in 1900, five years after the *Studies on Hysteria*. I am struck by

LORD JIM OR THE SHAME OF LIVING   135

the convergence concerning the search for the 'deep cause': Freud
was searching for the traumatic scene at the origin of the *neurotica*
in the hysteric. We know how this research would lead him first to
the incestuous seduction by the father, then to the fantasy of oedipal desire. The comparison is interesting with the 'psychic work'
which is accomplished between Marlow and Jim in order to reconstitute the 'original scene', and during which the issue of seduction
is central.

3. Conrad speaks later on of the 'convention present in every truth,
and of the essential sincerity of the lie'.

4. Marlow is first and foremost a narrative artifice—but has played a
crucial role in resolving Conrad's problem of writing. He doesn't
have a wife, or children, or any life of his own: he just needs to be
an old captain. His age allows him to offer a retrospective narration
over a long period, a narration addressed to old sailors; his compe-
tence authenticates the 'reality' of the facts. That Marlow does not
remain a pure narrator is somewhat troubling for the reader; but the
way in which he becomes party to the adventure makes the reader
sense intensely the extent of Conrad's involvement with Jim.

I note that Jim shamefully leaves the sea behind him to become
a hero on earth; and that Conrad left the Navy shortly after his first
command to become a great English writer. But this rupture also
marks the beginning of serious attacks of depression from which he
would suffer repeatedly, and which interfered greatly with his liter-
ary creation. To continue with the parallel, and without going into
the details of Conrad's life, it is worth recalling two crucial points
which throw light on the close bond between Conrad and Jim.

As we know, Conrad was the only son of Polish aristocrats who
fought against the Russian occupiers with heroic romanticism, in a
situation which scarcely left any place for realistic hope.

A first significant insight concerns the period when his father is
sent into exile in Russia: his wife and his son, aged 5, accompany
him. During this journey by sledge and this time spent in the North
of Russia where the wind blows constantly, Conrad's mother dies
of tuberculosis. He and his father—who never gets over it—are, as
it were, "survivors". We may wonder how much guilt, shared with
his 'helpless' father, this rescue/abandonment left him with?

The second insight concerns the period of adolescence. After
his father's death, Conrad finds himself, at the age of twelve, in
the position of a heroic orphan, destined to take the struggle for
Polish independence: the yoke of a transmitted idea and of its vital
menace. At the age of 16, in what may seem to be a way of *saving*

himself, or of *slipping away*, he leaves for Marseilles to become a sailor. The imputation of betrayal that came from his native country was to weigh on him for the rest of his life.

We can imagine what conflicts, what terrors, Jim constitutes as the return of the repressed, and what psychic work this *revenant* demands from Conrad. The writing of *Lord Jim*—via the mediation of Marlow—realizes the attempt at reincarnation and redemption of this *revenant*/survivor. The narrative process is pervaded entirely by the conflict of ambivalence between the desire to let Jim exist, to allow him an existential trajectory beyond the shipwreck which leaves him "guilty and done for", and the desire to make Jim vanish, to smother the story which threatens the author's "fragile egoism", his vulnerable spot.

5. Conrad suggests the possibility of the massive return of this core, even though the tissue of the book is made to contain it, and to only allow its return in a diffracted, reflected, drawn out form. Which is to say that writing itself seems to 'describe' the functioning of the psychic apparatus: a primary repression, constitutive of the interplay of repressions retroactively and of the returns of the repressed. Conrad's almost unbearable depth stems from the fact that he 'realizes' through and in writing the threat and promise of a lifting of all repression, a catastrophe through which the unconscious fantasy would be actualized in totality.

6. See Freud (1919) '"A Child is Being Beaten"', SE 17, 177–204.

7. Translator's note: an expression meaning an orgasm.

8. The second phase questions, crucially, the status of illusion/disillusion. Conrad expresses his ideas about this through the mouth of Stein, the man who Marlow sent Jim to see, and who gives Jim the opportunity for his glorious and tragic redemption. Stein suggests that man is a dreamer: any attempt to renounce dreams is as futile as trying to extract oneself from the unpleasant flood waters of life. The essential thing is not to struggle against the tidal waters, nor to let oneself drift, but to 'immerse oneself in the destructive element': an admirable metaphor which suggests both the status of the transitional area of illusion and the problematic of instinctual fusion inherent to primary masochism which is the guardian of psychic life.

References

Conrad, J. (1900). *Lord Jim*. (edited by Cedric Watts and Robert Hampson). London: Penguin, 1986.

CHAPTER SIX

Tender humour

B ecause it belongs principally to the spirit of thought, and
because the range of its manifestations can scarcely be reduced
to a *mechanism*, humour does not offer metapsychology the
same decisive holds as the joke. If Freud returned to it in a short
article of 1927, it was probably because he was not satisfied with
what he had said about it in his formidable work of 1905, *Jokes and
their Relation to the Unconscious*; but it was mainly because he had
a precise reason for doing so: he wanted to show that the point of
view of the second topography made it possible to account for it in
terms of the 'contribution made to the comic through the agency of
the Superego' (1927, 165). When I was asked to participate in this
edition of *Libres Cahiers*, I thought at first that I had nothing to add to
the article I had already published in the *Revue Française de Psychanalyse*: 'L'Humoriste et sa croyance' (Donnet, 1997). But I recalled the
joy I had had writing that paper, in spite of the formidable obstacles
encountered. It is true that, as humour is a theme that touches me
closely,[1] I had deeply identified with Freud. So I yielded to the temptation to revisit it, telling myself that, at the very least, I would be able
to clarify certain formulations that were previously too condensed.

* * *

137

When I took up Freud's very short text again, I had the same impression of incompleteness that I had had during my earlier readings. In spite of the crucial contribution made by the introduction of the Superego, Freud shows a certain reticence in approaching his subject. Thus, he emphasizes that it is with caution that psychoanalysis sets about the study of normal psychical processes, and that it is more secure in the field of pathology, whereas humour belongs to the domain of psychic health. But as he would do later in *Civilization and its Discontents* (1930), he puts it on the non hierarchical list of the modes of *regressive* functioning by means of which humanity tries to render life bearable for itself. Above all, by stressing the rareness not only of the capacity for the humorous attitude, but even of the capacity to enjoy it, he seems to want to limit the functional value of a practice that nonetheless had an important place, as we know, in his life and work. I think it is very likely that it was precisely his subjective predilection for humour—rather than for jokes—which prevented Freud from taking his ideas to their conclusion: his 'reticent' attitude is reminiscent of the attitude he displays elsewhere towards the artist.

It is true, however, that humour questions the theory of the Superego in a disturbing way: Freud (1927, p. 166) recognizes this clearly when he writes, 'If it is really the super-ego which, in humour, speaks such kindly words of comfort to the intimidated ego, this will teach us that we have still a great deal to learn about the nature of the super-ego'. It is not difficult, in fact, to note that humour raises the most crucial questions concerning the structuring of the Superego, questions that emerged in the wake of the metapsychological revisions of the 1920's. The first of these was the *new* pleasure principle and its articulation with the reality-principle, challenged by the question of illusion (1927 was the year of *The Future of an Illusion*); there was also the issue of the 'splitting of the Ego' (the article on 'Fetishism' is of the same year); and finally, and most importantly, there were the questions opened up by the text 'Negation' (1925). Freud's reservations in this short article may also be explained by the complexity and amplitude of the problems raised by the salubrious phenomenon of humour. The particular difficulty of exploring the subject in detail is that the reciprocal illumination that it involves reveals the obscurity which remains on each side.

* * *

Reduced to its essentials, the elucidation proposed by Freud comprises two indissociable aspects:

– the hypercathexis of the Superego modifies the endo-perception of the internal world; the massive activation of the comparison big/little—which, it will be recalled, is the general basis for the comic—makes the Ego *tiny* in relation to the magnified Superego.
– it changes the *apprehension* of the disagreeable situation, since the Superego, 'by repudiating reality, serves an illusion'. The Superego is the guardian of reality-testing by virtue of its origin in the parental agency, which, in its time, was *reality itself*. The menace which hangs over the Ego is *unrealized*, reduced to the inconsistency of an infantile fear; it is as though the Superego were saying to the Ego: 'Look! Here is the world, which seems so dangerous. It is nothing but a game for children—just worth making a jest about!' (1927, p. 166).

Thus resumed, the Freudian solution, in spite of its strength, seems rather schematic. Before attempting to include it within the complex dynamics of a *humoristic process*, it seems necessary to examine its conditions of possibility. Indeed, the very rareness of the capacity for humour suggests that it depends on the singular configuration of multiple factors. And why not begin with the astonishment that Freud seems to show with regard to the 'kindly words of comfort' that the Superego offers the Ego—comfort, however, which he links without hesitation to its origin in the parental agency? It is true that Freud places more emphasis on the Superego's predilection for cruelty, a predilection that has no direct relations with the *actual* behaviour of the parents, and which he explains in terms of the intensity of the struggle from which it has emerged and the instinctual defusion resulting from the desexualisation induced by the process of identification. But is this predilection not found in *black* humour, which is one of the most frequent registers of humour? It seems that Freud implicitly designates the presence of this concern as characterizing the very *essence* of the humoristic process: is it not this high point that confers pleasure with its exalting, liberating, *sublime* dimension? It is this completed, *ideal* form which I wish to focus on.

Its rareness no doubt reflects the customary difficulties of instinctual mitigation in Ego-Superego relations; and, of course, the temptation immediately arises to attribute its success to a *maternal* influence: is the smile of the Superego not that of the *Mona Lisa*? It seems natural to link this success to the most developed form of the Superego, the post-oedipal Superego, which Freud has just defined in *The Ego and the Id* (1923) as being constituted by two identifications, paternal and maternal, 'in some way united with each other' (p. 34). Humour thus finds one of its conditions of possibility in a particular mode of this preliminary agreement, in which the maternal image has its part to play. A *typical* form of this agreement is, for instance, the protective role played by the mother as a messenger of the threat of castration. The reminder of this protective and loving side of the Superego certainly contrasts for Freud with the exploration, required by clinical practice, of modes of relating between the Ego and the Superego, which, as in melancholia and moral masochism, only illustrate its cruel side. However, by emphasizing the bisexualization of the post-oedipal Superego, Freud implicitly designates it as the best bulwark against the threat of defusion. Why does he seem to hesitate to recognize the maternal influence in the genesis of humoristic pleasure? Perhaps he mistrusts what he designates as a 'consolation?'

We would do well to recall his warning in *Civilization and its Discontents* against the 'nurses lullaby song' which makes of man—of the phallic hero?—a *lulled*, and thus *deluded* child. In fact, the success of *tender* humour makes Freud inquire more deeply into the evolution that he has assigned to the Superego, and in particular to the privilege conferred on its impersonalisation. I want to raise certain aspects of this problem, which I have discussed elsewhere, (Donnet, 2008) with reference to the crucial text on 'The Economic Problem of Masochism' (1924). In fact, at the same time as he identifies in this text the principle of a structural primary and secondary masochism, required by the hypothesis of the death drive and the demand for fusion underlying the *new* pleasure principle, Freud is led by the formidable obstacle of the negative therapeutic reaction to describe moral masochism in a particularly menacing light; the insistence on its acted, perverse register makes him overlook the existence of a *normal* masochistic dimension at work in Ego-Superego relations which is part of the economy of masochism as the 'guardian of psychic life' (B. Rosenberg, 1991) When he designates the regressive resexualisation specific to moral masochism, Freud is referring to female masochism, but he traces it back it immediately to a pregenitality which telescopes the oppositions masculine/feminine, phallic/castrated, active/passive, and, as a result, overlooks the virtuality of a *feminized* masochism that could play a role between Superego and Ego. To be sure, Freud's position is a response to an urgent clinical preoccupation; but, on the one hand it is marked by its subjective repugnance for those 'who commit sin in order to derive pleasure from expiation' (cf. 'Dostoyevsky and Parricide', 1928); and, on the other, he is embarrassed by the univocal meaning that he gives to the term resexualization, without considering the new extension that is conferred upon it by the duality Eros/death drives.[2] It is clear, then, that Freud primarily detects in Ego-Superego relations the double menace of the Superego's sadism and the Ego's masochism, while leaving to one side the question of the Ideal. Consequently, the delicate issue of the progressive and necessary impersonalisation of the Superego is raised in a unilateral way. In fact, only a *radical* impersonalisation would be a sign of the true *destruction* of the Oedipus complex, a destruction that would prohibit resexualisation-repersonalisation, henceforth reserved exclusively for moral masochism. However, in an eloquent formulation concluding his description of the Superego, Freud (1924, p. 168) recognizes that 'only the fewest of us are able to look upon [the figures of destiny] as impersonal'; which amounts to saying that it is not difficult to detect in each person's relations with these 'ultimate and remotest' figures the persistence of imaginary libidinal ties which turn them into substitutes for oedipal objects. It must therefore be accepted that the idea of a radical and irreversible impersonalisation is only a fiction which is linked with that of a pure symbolic order without any imaginary content.

Having made this observation, we are bound to recognize that the Ego-Superego relation is the support of a *regressive potential whose effects can be for the best or the worst. Normally* this capacity participates in the narcissistic—particularly moral—equilibrium. In reaction to the crises of life and the ordeals of destiny, the regressive reactivation of the origins of the Superego constitutes a structural recourse whose explicit appeal to the religious is only the manifest, recognized form.

The desirable trend towards impersonalisation-desexualisation is not incompatible with the employment of this regressive capacity, which, incidentally, is inherent to the recognition of the Superego as an agency (Donnet, 2005). The psychopathology of everyday life offers a very large range of phenomena involving this regressive capacity, showing how the Superego remains indefinitely capable of projection, repersonalisation, and resexualisation in many diverse and nuanced modes, as is illustrated by the analytic transference.

* * *

Humour evinces a particularly complex and subtle use of this capacity. Two conditions emerge from what precedes: first, a mode of instinctual mitigation which rests on a truly post-phallic bisexualisation of the Superego, sustaining the virtuality of a certain type of relation between the Superego and the Ego; and secondly, the structuring of a reality principle in which the Superego has played a supportive role. In effect, Freud underlines the importance of the double origin of the Superego, which has emerged both from the Id, since the introjected objects were instinctually cathected objects, and from the external world, since these objects constituted an essential part of reality. This double origin provides a model for the Ego in its task of conciliating the demands of the Id and reality. The humorist must have traces of such a model in order to play on the ambiguity of the relations between the pleasure principle and the reality principle.[3] Thus by going back towards the origins of the Superego, the regressive process can involve simultaneously the primary maternal object and the register of primary illusion. This concomitance no doubt throws light on the astonishment and reserved attitude of Freud, who, in his text, only refers to the identification with the Father, and seems a little reticent about the way that 'the Superego serves an illusion'. It is true that humour *conjures up* the themes of the denial of reality and ego-splitting, described at the same time with regard to fetishism.[4]

I hope I have said enough about the conditions of the humoristic process to throw light on the reasons for its rareness, and to support a more detailed approach to its dynamics.

* * *

I will begin with two lines of inquiry which illustrate the complexity of the phenomenon:

1. The first concerns the place of the *jest*. Freud is not absolutely clear on this subject. It does not seem to be an integral part of

humour insofar as it is only a *preliminary*, he says, the main point of which lies in the intention it serves, and thus in the frame of mind, one might say, the subjective position adopted. Unlike the joke in which the listener, the 'third person', plays a structural role, humour can do without the spectator. Freud notes that its process can unfold entirely within the humorist himself, and that this is probably the most original and most essential form of humour. It is this form of humour that I will be focusing on. It is significant here that Freud takes as his starting-point what happens in the *spectator* to remind us of the major characteristic of humour: identifying himself with the humorist who finds himself faced with an unpleasant situation, this spectator anticipates the corresponding painful feelings, which he is *spared* (humour was first defined as *spared or economised feelings*); however, by *copying* the humorist, the spectator also shares the qualitative transformation of the spared feelings. Freud thus suggests that a deep understanding of the humoristic process occurs through direct, empathic identification with the humorist, which implies, I think, that one of the registers of the process belongs to the unrepresentable, to 'shared affect' (C. Parat, 1998). How, then, are the participation of the spectator and the function of the jest that is addressed to him to be understood? If the *flash of humour* gives rise to a story, the jest is necessary for its listener and readily takes the form of a joke. But what about the direct spectator of the humorist 'in a real-life situation'? My answer would be that he is there as an *indefinite other*, to serve as a *witness*, a witness to the fact that the humorist does not need him, and does not address any complaint to him; he is only there to attest to the humorist's self-sufficiency; as for the jest, which objectifies the success of what is happening in the humorist's mind, it affords the witness a bonus of pleasure which allows him to be sufficiently *in on it* to feel that he is an *accomplice* in the face of *nasty* reality. But his admiration, even if it is better assured, is not necessary for the humorist's pleasure.

2. The second line of questioning concerns the place of language in the humoristic process itself. It will have been noted that Freud puts a 'discourse' into the mouth of the Superego: 'Look! Here is the world, which seems so dangerous. It is nothing but a game for children— just worth making a jest about!' He thus evokes an internal dialogue between the agencies.[5] We know how important

the *internal voice* of the Superego is, as well as the weight of word-presentations in its functioning; but for Freud, its instinctual register ultimately remains prevalent. Moreover, the *discourse* addressed here to the Ego appears awkward, inadequate, as if Freud were obliged to *put into dialogue* that which is at play beyond words. I am particularly struck by the words 'it is nothing but a game for children': certainly the expression used in its metaphorical sense is pertinent, but it appears rather strange while speaking to a tiny Ego, to the child in the humorist. The expression is striking, especially as, in describing the wooden reel game, Freud showed the depth and gravity of the implications of the child's play. I wonder if Freud's formulation was not unconsciously affected by the comparison that imposes itself between the play of humour and a child's play. The recourse to a verbal formulation would correspond to a need to render *expressible* a processual phenomenon whose direct access, as I have emphasized, seems to involve a primary identification that is ultimately incompatible with the register of representation.

However, it is true that the humoristic process itself needs words, and that it needs a counterpoint to what happens in the field of the massive displacements of cathexes on which Freud places so much emphasis. We can assume that the internal dialogue[6] resembles the dialogue with which the child *accompanies* the scenario of its play, using several voices, with their respective intonations. It must be distinguished from the jest: the latter, which can be minimal and amount to no more than a gesture or facial expression, must, in the last resort, indicate that the unpleasant situation is *present* in a pleasant way. It only has an indirect relation with the representations of affects and words which mark the process. It uses the power that the symbol of negation offers to freedom of thought: in this sense, it functions as a counter-cathexis, at the same time as a 'starter'.[7]

Humoristic speech translates into words an *ingenuous* mode of thinking, with an innocence that is unaware of inhibition or censorship; it is often evocative of a *child's remark*, a child who knows he can say anything he likes with impunity.[8]

* * *

These insights into the ambiguous status of the spectator and language in the humoristic process suffice, I think, to avoid the temptation of conceiving humour as the effect of a lure of the Superego, a lure made possible by the simple hypercathexis of the agency, producing a sort of temporary illusion. In fact, at the end of the process, the humorist experiences no disillusionment; he is always ready to face the situation of reality that he has never left.[9] The complexity of a sufficiently detailed understanding of the process stems from the fact that the regression it involves implies simultaneously the optimal use of the instruments of the Ego; in addition, this regression operates both in a primary and secondary identificatory register— the internal dialogue between several voices—and in the register of a relation of an anaclitic type. It must be assumed that the enactment of humour solicits the whole of the process of *superegoization* from its origin in the primary object to its post-oedipal completion in symbolic impersonalisation; and that each of the vicissitudes of this structuring plays its part in what permits or prevents access to humoristic pleasure in its diverse shades. I have pointed out that this process is never completed, and that it can therefore ideally support the regressive and progressive movements involved in the process of humour.

* * *

How can the dynamics of the humoristic process be described while acknowledging this complexity? The movement of the hypercathexis of the Superego referred to by Freud is fundamental, but the question that immediately arises concerns the evolution of this first displacement. It thus seems necessary to me to integrate within the process the *recuperation* by the Ego of this cathexis which it initially abandoned. I would like to suggest that humoristic pleasure stems from the way in which the recuperation occurs, by sustaining the deployment and decondensation of the *fantasies* potentially contained in the initial economic hypercathexis of the Superego. My description thus implies a movement back and forth between the Ego and the Superego. The two currents—which I am describing here as successive—are in fact simultaneous, realizing a two-way *circulation* with different rhythms of flow and regressive and progressive stages. To do justice to the deepest resonance of humour, it is necessary to postulate that the massive movements of cathexes referred to by Freud reproduce earlier movements which have contributed to the structuring itself of the agencies of the psychical apparatus; for humour seems in the last resort to be a celebration of the auto-erotic capacity for thinking, a condensed form of the history of a subjectivized pleasure principle.

From this perspective, the first phase can be described as an auto-decathexis of the Ego which allows it to make use of *its* Superego regressively; this displacement owes the quality of its impact to the fact that it is a *replication* of the inaugural moment of the institution of the oedipal Superego. The essential aim of this was to protect the Ego against the danger linked to the threat of castration. The desexualizing internalization of the oedipal objects contributed to the instinctual repression and, as a result, eliminated the danger that they represented both by their attraction and their menace. Humour, by repeating on the *internal scene* what was originally a largely *constrained* institution, confirms and reaffirms its seductive and narcissizing register. By actualizing this instituting phase, the Ego *resuscitates* the Superego which was not yet differentiated from the hypercathected objects that were being introjected, and which combined in its original double the Id and reality: so the Ego corresponds to the Superego *model* described by Freud.

The child, as a humorist, might say, 'Nothing can happen to me'. However, it evokes less the humorist's attitude of concern and consolation than his position of grandiosity and invulnerability. But this position scarcely corresponds to the decathexis of a *tiny* Ego; this is where Freud's allusion to an identification of the Ego with the Superego is justified—an identification linked to the father, as usual! There are thus grounds for taking into consideration an *identificatory regression* of the Ego involving a quasi-hallucinatory animistic register: the feeling of grandiosity thus reflects *directly* the magnitude of the cathexis as it emerges from the contrast big/little. The characteristic ambivalence of identification throws light on the nature of the challenge, of the triumph contained in the pleasure experienced. This identification constitutes *one* of the modes of recovering the consented hypercathexis: the humorist is really not a child who sees misfortune as an opportunity for being consoled! He seems rather to possess a narcissistic assurance concerning which one may wonder if it is based only on the recourse/return to a dependency on oedipal objects whose internalization he plays out again. It is necessary, perhaps, to invoke the original situation where the very notion of dependency on the object did not obtain: a phase of symbiotic functioning, of complete power over the still undifferentiated all-powerful Other. The humorist's *confidence* reflects the immanent *certitude* of having the Other unconditionally at his disposal: the Other of the primary identification 'prior to any object choice'. It is significant that Freud refers here, precisely, to a Superego that is the 'core of the Ego' and it will be recalled that, for him, the oedipal identifications of the Superego simply *reinforce* the primary identifications.[10] The unrepresentable dimension of the regressive process corresponds to the implication of this narcissistic basis detected by Freud in 'An Introduction to Narcissism' (1914), when he refers to the fascination that the humorist exerts in the same way as the great criminal![11]

Freud was not wrong when he said that humour questions the Superego in its very essence, and that we should not yield to the temptation to simply appeal to the maternal voice in spite of the somewhat misleading reference to the *'kindly words of comfort'*; such words are nothing other than the reversal of the original presence of the sadistic *mockery* characteristic of the comic.

* * *

Does the identification of the Ego with the magnified Superego suffice to explain the process? No, because its *magic* character does not explain the range and the nuanced mixture of the affects which make up the complexity of humoristic pleasure. The Ego owes its capacity to disinvest itself and to recreate its Superego to the intangibility of its narcissistic foundations; but this same intangibility also assures the second phase of the process in which the Ego shows that it is capable of disinvesting the Superego in its turn, of *detaching itself from it, just as it detached itself from its oedipal objects by virtue of its institution*. It is clear that, faced with the frustrating situation, the interest of the process is twofold: the assurance of re-finding the omnipotent object goes hand in hand with that of being in a position to do without it. The humorist's pleasure contains the ingredient of de-idealization. And we can understand better how the humorist's narcissism makes minimal use of the witness as object: it is the support of a relative externalization of the Superego which must collude with its effacement, just as the object, at one time, effaced itself at the right moment, making a gift of its absence. In actual fact, it seems to me that it is the Ego which *lures* its Superego by making it believe in its omnipotence. The Superego 'serves an illusion', but it is the Ego that creates it to assure itself that it fears no disillusionment. The humorist's pleasure is derived, in the last resort, from the recuperation by the Ego of its initial hypercathexis of the Superego. We can see why this recuperation must not take place via the *short* path of identification alone: pleasure would switch into a moment of mania—fusion of the Ego and the Superego—whose euphoria would be *deceptive*, whereas it is discretely marked by the *depressive position* and the anticipation of mourning. The recuperation must therefore take place slowly and be restrained by a flexible counter-cathexis; the continuous path of the cathexis implies that the displacement occurs quickly in the regressive direction of the hypercathexis of the Superego, and slowly in the progressive direction of recuperation by the Ego. What is important is that at the end of this two-way process, the Ego conserves the narcissistic benefit of a regression which has occurred *in its service*. The weak intensity of the experience is the consequence of this dynamic which *holds back* and *distils* the discharge: in other words, it is a smile rather than hearty laughter. But, by way of compensation, its pleasure can be extended and savoured—like a good wine with a 'lingering finish', which *delivers* a series of savours and aromas in a harmonious mixture. At the end, it melts into a personal and private joy of thinking.

* * *

Owing to the slowness of the recuperation, the Ego can introduce into the relationship it *negotiates* with its Superego the significant fantasmatic ideas relating to the history of its introjections, without undermining the status of the agency. The humorist thus makes use of, and *plays* with, the ambiguity of the relations that the superego function entertains with the reality principle. There is, for example, in the humorist's defiance, in his invulnerability, a certain proximity with the figure of the hero. This theme could correspond to the resurgence of an oedipal moment in which the unpleasant reality *was* the figure of the castrating father; the support that the humorist finds, then, in his Superego, could be the equivalent of maternal complicity: an illustration of the interference between the double origin of the Superego and the vicissitudes of the Oedipus complex. On the other hand, at the end of a process of recuperation, during which the Ego has restored to the Superego its impersonal nature, the humorist unites his two parents; he has now appropriated his *primal scene*, thereby reconciling the painful recognition of the reality of his origin and a more assured affirmation of his narcissistic foundations. The sequencing of these scenarios presupposes that they remain moderately and fleetingly cathected, under the aegis of Eros binding the aggression of auto-sadism. The pleasure principle only celebrates its extension by losing its intensity, by attenuating the conflictuality of the principles of functioning. The attractive force of black humour, of derision, of biting irony, like the increased intensity of the discharge that they provoke, clearly shows that the *tender* humour which I am speaking of here results from the *rare*, maximal fusion of the drives of destruction to which bisexualization has made its contribution, thereby bearing witness to the success of an erogenous life masochism.

* * *

Unlike the joke, which aims at pleasure alone, or the satisfaction of the aggressive tendency, humour, Freud notes, does not satisfy any instinctual impulse. 'But,' he stresses, 'without rightly knowing why, we regard this less intense pleasure as having a character of very high value' (1927, p. 166). I would even say that it has *the very savour of value*, bearing in mind what he says in *Civilization and its Discontents*, 'our judgements of value follow directly from our wishes for happiness and that they are accordingly an attempt to support illusions' (p. 145). The sense of exaltation felt by the humorist—and by his spectator—is the sublime itself, insofar as, first of all, it is simply a quality of experience: a sensation of lightness and relief which is *uplifting*. The greatness of the humorist is to manifest the triumph of the pleasure principle on the terrain of frustrating reality; one could say in the very exercise of the reality principle. But what is the relationship between this narcissistic experience and the *value*, the *elevation* of thought which accompanies it? Freud insists that the depth and wisdom of the thought content *play no part* in the pleasure; and yet it seems to derive capital out of it, as if the regressive technique enhanced its significance; as if the form reconciled the thought content with the adversity of the world. It is necessary to go even further: sometimes only the humoristic procedure is capable of rendering the horror or the obscene *thinkable*; in the book on jokes, Freud noted that this was why humour had always fascinated the *Thinkers*. This aptitude for broadening the field of what is thinkable questions the very *origin* of thought. Humour is related to the power of negation, to the freedom it offers thought to free itself from the constraint of the pleasure principle. But humour maintains this principle by preserving the freedom to think. Refusing the idea that the judgement of existence replaces the judgement of attribution, he reaffirms the foundational precession of the second over the first. For this to be the case, the regressive activation of his Superego must combine the lack of differentiation characteristic of its preobjectal anchoring and the impersonalisation characteristic of its post-oedipal destiny. On the one hand, the absolute weapon of omnipotent animism appeals to the *Ideal Ego*—a *purified pleasure-Ego*, made possible by the care of the Superego;[12] on the other, the humorist's intact lucidity is based on an Ego-Ideal which makes him invest the exercise of a *pure* reality principle: it is because he distinguishes clearly between reality principle and pleasure principle that the humorist can play on their interference and subvert the first. If the regressive capacity is to be able to sustain the movements of desexualization and sexualization characteristic of the sublimatory process, a particular impersonalisation of the superego agency is necessary.

In this respect, the position of the humorist is symmetrical and converse to that of the moral masochist. The latter is always obliged to project his Superego in order to find, behind hard reality, the sexualized figure of the *Father who beats*; he has to confer a punitive intention on the figures of Destiny and an expiatory meaning on events. The humorist, on the other hand, believes in *pure chance*; like the poet Multatoli whom Freud mentions, he only sees in the figures of destiny the pair Reason and Necessity. So he only makes a *strictly internal* use of his Superego; the vicissitudes of reality are for him an *opportunity* to prove to himself that 'he does not need anyone' in order to love himself and to feel loved. But, by virtue of the psychic exploit that he accomplishes, the humorist is not so very different, at his level, from the creative artist and his transgressive act.

Notes

1. Was it not of me that it was said, when I was young: 'for a good joke, he would kill father and mother?'
2. The investments of the Ego after the constitution of secondary narcissism must be considered as pertaining to the sexualization

characteristic of Eros; the same is true for sublimation. Cf J.-L. Baldacci, 'Dès le début ... la Sublimation?' Report to the Congress of French-Speaking Psychoanalysts, 2004, *Revue française de psychanalyse*, vol 69(5), 2005, pp. 1405ff.

3. This prefigures what is at stake in Winnicottian transitionality.
4. In this respect, the most immediate difference between the humorist and the fetishist is that the 'splitting of the ego' corresponds in the first to an actively variable and conflictual functional differentiation, whereas in the second there is a partial and fixed alteration of the Ego. Freud only refers briefly, in the *Outline*, to the relations between these two forms of splitting, relations which are not unconnected with the doubt that he expresses at the beginning of the article on 'The Splitting of the Ego in the Process of Defence' (1940 [1938]) as to the novelty of the concept. The split between the Ego and the Superego is thus assumed to be a normal prototype whose flexible functioning could *prevent* subsequent pathological splitting.
5. Francis Pasche (1969) placed a lot of emphasis on this dimension of the relations between the agencies of the psychical apparatus.
6. It would be interesting to compare it with the 'internal discourse' as it is conceptualised by Jean-Claude Rolland in *Avant d être celui qui parle*, Paris: Gallimard, 2005.
7. In English in the original.
8. I will return to the example I gave in 1998: a little girl, aged 5, has just learnt of the existence of death, and it makes her think; snuggling up in her mother's arms, she asks: ' Mummy, I know that everyone has to die, but will Daddy necessarily die at the same time as you?'
9. The humorist is not in an auto-hypnotic state. However, in *Group Psychology and the Analysis of the Ego*, Freud reminds us that by projecting his *Superego-Ideal* on to the hypnotiser, the hypnotic subject delegates reality testing to him. In *The Ego and the Id*, three years later, he points out in a note that it was by mistake that he had attributed reality-testing to the Superego, since it is a function of the Ego. This uncommented rectification clearly points up the acuity of the metapsychological problem that humour illustrates in a crucial way.
10. One could also refer to a primordial reciprocal seduction.
11. I am also thinking here of the 'Double' as it appears in 'The Uncanny' (1919): The humorist's Ego coincides with the primordial *good double*, while the *bad double* emerges from the first refusals of reality and coincides with the cruel Superego.
12. In 'The Two Principles of Mental Functioning' (SE 12, 220), Freud writes : 'The employment of a fiction like this however justified

when one considers that the infant—provided one includes with it the care it receives from its mother—does almost realize a psychical system of this kind.'

References

Donnet, J.-L. (1997). 'L'Humoriste et sa croyance'. *Revue Française de Psychanalyse*, *61*(3): pp. 897–917.

Donnet, J.-L. (2005). 'Le Surmoi et les transformations du complexe d'Oedipe', *Libres Cahiers,12*, Autumn 2005.

Donnet, J.-L. (2008). 'Le père et l'impersonnalisation du Surmoi. In *Hommage à André Green. Figures modernes du père*. Paris: Presses Universitaires de France.

Freud, S. (1905). *Jokes and their Relation to the Unconscious, SE*, 8.

Freud, S. (1924). *The Economic Problem of Masochism. SE 19*: 155–170.

Freud, S. (1927). *Humour. SE*, *21*: 160–166.

Freud, S. (1928). *Dostoevsky and Parricide. SE*, *21*: 177–196.

Freud, S. (1940 [1938]). *The Splitting of the Ego in the Process of Defence. SE*, *23*: 271–278.

Parat, C. (1998). *Affect partagé*. Paris: Presses Universitaires de France.

Pasche, F. (1969). *A partir de Freud*. Paris: Payot.

Rosenberg, B. (1991). 'Le masochisme mortifère et masochisme gardien de la vie'. In *Le Masochisme*, Monograph, *Revue Psychanalyse Française*, Presses Universitaires de France.

CHAPTER SEVEN

Freud and the shadow of the superego[1]

If there is a Freudian concept that evokes the idea of heritage and its shadow, it is the concept of the superego. The very term indicates that, by towering above the Ego, the Superego casts a shadow that is either threatening or protective. The notion of heritage brings together the key issues of *disappearance* and transmission, of legacy and usufruct.

The creation of the superego in 1923 marks a crucial step in Freud's thought, but his formulations concerning it are often as contradictory as they are profound. The most perspicacious research in the Freudian heritage has often needed to draw on a clarified, but also narrowly delimited and functional Freudian concept—the so-called post-Oedipal Superego. However, the *Freudian project* of the superego is valuable because of its very ambiguities, reflecting its fundamentally paradoxical character (Donnet, 1995). Rather than identifying the references in it, I have chosen to re-read in the light of our theme a late, brief, self-analytical text over which the shadow of the superego hangs.

* * *

153

'It seems as though the essence of success was to have got further than one's father, and as though to excel one's father was still something [not permitted[2]].' This is how Freud (1936, p. 247) summarizes, in his letter to Romain Rolland, the results of the analysis he offers him in 'A Disturbance of Memory on the Acropolis' (1936). The interpretation of the episode was put off for many years, as it goes back to 1904. By emphasizing that a whole a *generation* separated him from this date, Freud (1936, p. 239) undoubtedly gave us the key to what had made the elucidation of a phenomenon whose memory had 'kept on recurring to [his] mind' over 'the last few years' possible: he was old, sickly and unable to travel, and he required indulgence, just like the de-idealized father he had evoked. Was this identification, reactivated by death's proximity, not necessary to interpret the subjective enigma that was at that point left unresolved?

* * *

It will be recalled that the estrangement on the Acropolis was preceded by a more discrete episode experienced in Trieste, after the two brothers had suddenly had the possibility of visiting Athens rather than Corfu as they had planned. While they were strolling about in Trieste, they were overcome by depressed spirits, and their discussion only turned around the obstacles that seemingly stood in the way of their plans. However, when the moment arrived, the two brothers turned up without hesitation at the Lloyd's booking office in order to board the boat departing for Piraeus. Freud interprets the previous experience as a typical manifestation of what is 'too good to be true' (1936, p. 242) which expresses the paradoxical denial of a pleasant reality. He writes: 'the internal frustration commands him to cling to the external one' (p. 242): the vexation of the evoked mood corresponds very well to the felt frustration owing to the fact that the thing is impossible. Freud insists on the frequent pessimistic attitude which makes one think: 'one cannot expect Fate to grant one anything so good' (p. 242). In fact, it is a matter of the manifestation of a feeling of guilt or inferiority which may be thus expressed, 'I'm not worthy of such happiness, I don't deserve it' (p. 242). For 'the Fate which we expect to treat us so badly is a materialization of our conscience, of the severe superego within us, itself a residue of the punitive agency of our childhood' (p. 243).

Freud makes the incidence of the superego the interpretative key of the two episodes but, in analyzing his estrangement, he simply emphasizes that the same *incredulity* towards what, in principle, is a pleasant piece of reality manifests itself in Trieste and on the Acropolis, and that the difference stems from what distinguishes a simple possibility from its realization. The *presence* of the desired object accounts for the fact that the *perceptive* register is directly *touched*; however, Freud does not make it clear how the effect of the superego exerts itself. I refer the reader to my addendum for a precise reading of Freud's text and its difficulties. I just want to emphasize here that the pleasure of delight and *exaltation* expected by Freud implied the delicate conjunction between the well-informed contemplation of the site and the activation of his private imagination with regard to Greek antiquity. My hypothesis is that it was disturbed by the irruptive actualization of the animistic ways of thinking of the adolescent. This throws light on the complexity of the sense of malaise and Freud's difficulty in discerning the specific incidence of the superego in it. In Trieste, the internal frustration originating in the superego concerns representations: it *clings* projectively to *fictive* obstacles of reality; an internal, hysterical scene of disappointment enables the ego to delude the superego in order to maintain its mastery over the act. On the Acropolis, an experience of enjoyment activates perception. Faced with the seductive solicitation of the site, a telescoping may have taken place between the pressure of the Id-impulses and the condemnation of the superego. The introduction of the Superego is translated by two contradictory effects: the derealization which reflects the decathexis of what has been perceived spoils the subject's pleasure, but spares him the hallucinatory *surreality*, which is implicitly designated by the reference to the Loch Ness Monster. The deep truth of the formulation, 'So all this really *does* exist, just as we learnt at school!' (p. 241), is that it refers the Ego to the factuality of the ruins alone. The disturbance on the Acropolis calls into question what Freud calls the sense of reality and the possible role played by the superego in it. I shall return to this point.

In his final interpretation, Freud explains what made the trip to Athens a transgressive act. The desire to travel has its origin in adolescent rebellion, and the wish to escape the paternal home, the narrowness of the environment, and the limitations of its poverty. This desire contains a violent de-idealizing of the father, following his initial idealization. Embarking for Athens, which concretizes its accomplishment, thus indissolubly connects that which incites action and what, from the inside, marks it with the stamp of what is impermissible. Freud adds that the fact that 'Athens could not have meant much' (p. 247) to his father was the source of a movement of piety which might help to overcome feelings of rivalry. The discovery of Athens was moreover linked to the extension of old sublimatory cathexes to which the knowledge of Greek civilization belonged. And these cathexes could not have occurred if he had not indirectly received the support from a father who, like most fathers, hoped that his sons would go *further* on the path of life. If the decision to embark was taken without hesitation or discussion, it was because it was sustained by the function of an object of the ideal. Freud's aphorism immediately begs the question of the relationship between the Superego and the Ideal, which I shall return to shortly.

But the journey to Athens is also and primarily a metaphor for life's journey, of the path that the ego must trace in order to become a subject.[3] The aphorism is thus striking due to its radicalism. True, it only concerns what is essential in success, what, in the last resort, qualifies it psychically. But it nonetheless asserts that all success, because its *attraction* owes *something* to the desire '*to go further than the father*', and because it remains oriented towards a primordial identificatory rivalry, is affected by an element of guilt. The result is that the shadow of the superego haunts all success, and the sublimatory value, the metaphorical dimension, the gap created by the symbolic displacement is unable to efface the trace of the originary impetus. The agency of the superego, by its very existence, perpetuates this *fixation*. Here we are touching on a major ambiguity in the Freudian superego: the progressive nature and irreversibility of the psychic transformations of which it is at once the effect and the cause. I shall only mention here certain aspects of its metapsychology, *those which by designating it as 'heir', can throw light on the enigmatic dimension of the aphorism.*

The intra-psychic presence of an active conflictual rivalry initially reflects a superego identificatory *nucleus*. If Freud makes the superego an agency, it is in order to assert that the identifications constituting it are no more capable of being integrated into the Ego in their totality than the Id. Their most specific character is that, originating in the internalization of objects on which the infant is vitally dependent, they exercise a restraining, alienating power over the ego: in this sense they correspond to the 'melancholic' model of narcissistic identification. The establishment of the superego thus constitutes 'a loan with great consequences', a debt that can never be paid: such is the deeply identificatory otherness underlying the feeling operating in all success that something is 'impermissible'. By contrast, Freud describes the later identifications of a strengthened Ego: it introjects them by assimilating them into itself; they no longer dominate it because they correspond to the model of symbolic, hysterical identification. The dynamic and economic organization of these identifications forms part of the long process of 'superegoization' stretching from the oedipal period into adulthood. In effect, the Oedipal identifications are already seen as compatible with the maintenance of affectionate object cathexes, which relativizes their hold on the ego. As to the notion of the superego as 'heir to the Oedipal complex', it turns out to be extremely ambiguous. Freud is not very clear as to the status of the *disappearance of the Oedipus complex*, and in particular the irreversibility of the transformations it implies. Normative evolution towards a relative impersonalization is above all accompanied by the opening of the Superego-Ideal to new models of identification, far from the Oedipal objects. This progressive evolution might make one doubt the structural significance of the aphorism. Nevertheless, Freud maintains that the superego 'tends to perpetuate the conditions which gave birth to it', that is, the infantile dependence of the Ego, while contending that the task of the ego is to 'escape from the superego's authority'. It stems from this that, from a Freudian point of view, the most significant result of the end of the Oedipal period is the creation of an Ego-Superego differentiation *within the Ego*. In order to do justice to the ambiguity of this formulation, one could say that the Superego is an heir which continues indefinitely to establish its rights, whereas the Ego strives to appropriate the inheritance for itself. The play of reversals in the identificatory positions that the ego-superego split makes possible throws light on the paradox that the realization of the Ego's identificatory desire must involve the sense of having transgressed.

* * *

The notion of a superego nucleus puts into question the dual-heir status of the Superego-Ideal. In fact, Freud uses the term 'heir' twice.

In *Group Psychology* (1921), he makes the Ego-Ideal the heir of primary narcissism and he emphasizes the ease with which, in many individuals, the Ego takes itself for the Ideal in an unreal manner. In *The Ego and the Id* (1923), the superego is the ambiguous heir of the Oedipus complex. It is beginning with this duality that the narcissistic line of the Ideal has been opposed, in a way that is often fruitful, to the object line of the Superego. But Freud insists above all on the dual origin of the Superego itself, in the Id and in reality: in fact, the Oedipal objects, which it originates in, were intensely cathected by the Id; and they also constituted an essential part of reality. This is why Freud does not separate the Superego and the Ego-Ideal, and attributes to the Superego the function of the Ideal inseparable from the organization of a secondary narcissism and the sexualized object cathexes it presupposes. The notion of function implies that the Ego strives *to return* to its Ideal in order to restore a lost narcissistic completeness but without ever coinciding with it—except occasionally. Is not one of the tasks of the Superego precisely to watch over and guarantee this gap protecting the function of desire. And it is not because a project is true to the Ideal that its realization should not revive any trace of internal conflict. Freud does not say that it is *forbidden (interdit)* to surpass the father;[4] he merely says that it is not permitted. Should we not recognize that any project involving the Ego-Ideal implies the transgression of a limit? Transgression, because it does not wait for *permission*, must assume the psychic cost of acting out. I have suggested that, on the Acropolis, Freud found himself exposed to the alternative between a narcissistic regression to the Ideal-Ego and the mourning which so often marks wish-fulfillment.

It is also due to its dual origin that the Superego must, according to Freud, serve as the Ego's model for the relationship between the Id and reality. For, as it has become a part of the inner world, in intimate relation with the Id, the Superego continues to assume the role of an external reality. In thus bringing together inside and outside, it intervenes directly in the structuring of the reality principle. In *Group Psychology*, Freud even attributed the function of reality testing to the Superego-ideal: at the time he was prompted by the fact that the hypnotizer who has replaced the Superego possesses the power of dictating his perceptive reality onto the hypnotized subject. In *The Ego and the Id*, Freud rectifies his *error* by attributing reality testing to the Ego. But is the *rectification* of this projective error, or illusion, not an ordinary and indefinite task of the Ego faced with the regressive temptation to place reality under the sign of a principle which would be 'the principle of an Other's pleasure', of 'the Other'? What is involved, after all, is the problem of transference. This issue was present in Freud's symptom: in Trieste, the Superego's reprobation was transformed into a hostility of destiny, the 'not permitted' into 'not possible'. This projective movement reverses the movement of introjection, which, while the Superego is establishing itself, sustains secondary narcissism by substituting the inner interdiction for a real impotency. The superego's projection onto the figures of destiny makes it possible to relocate the malevolent or benevolent parental objects on the outside.

In 'The Economic Problem of Masochism' (1924), Freud emphasized the rarity of a complete impersonalization of the figures of destiny. In fact, such an impersonalization—closely related to a symbolic function freed of all imaginary content—is a lure: the Ego-Superego differentiation possesses, thanks to its splitting, a regressive capacity which authorizes, for better or worse, the reestablishment of a more or less subdued animistic relationship with the outside world. The most salubrious example of putting this regressive capacity into play is the subjective position of the humorist, so dear to Freud. On the other hand, on the Acropolis, the hostility of his Superego contributed to the feeling of the unreality of his inner vision. Winnicott's concept of *transitional phenomena* has shed light on the important issue of an animistic cathexis of reality in which the object plays a crucial role, and which turns out to be fundamental to the structuring experience of illusion-disillusionment.

The superego may also freely share itself in order to structure a group. The journey to Athens implied the collusion of the two brothers. The scene in Trieste unfolds in a theatre that is at once internal and intersubjective, and the fraternal complicity has its role in the silent decision and the climate of fear *they both shared*. *Brotherhood* thus constitutes a mini-group in which each identifies with the other through the same Ideal, and the same *enemy*.[5] The Superego's implication thus also brings out the trans-subjective dimension, and more so its tie to the cultural superego of the time. It goes without saying that a cross-generational dimension finds itself enacted by the *rivalry* between Greek and Jewish cultures.[6] Lastly, on the phylogenic level, the brothers' complicity cannot be mentioned without evoking the murder of the father and the myth of *Totem and Taboo* (1912–1913): another, cross-generational heritage of the superego.

Freud's aphorism obliges us to gauge the obscurity attached to the notion of a fixed superego nucleus. He appears to refer, in the last resort, to the abutment of primary identification, *prior* to any object choice. Freud thinks that the secondary oedipal identifications reinforce the primary identifications. It seems to me rather that the long process of the superego's establishment (*surmoïsation*) implies a profound and continuous alteration of the identifications and their very status. This process is buttressed on the primary nucleus by relativizing its effects without integrating or dissolving the *sediment*, the *precipitate* in it. In consequence, the Ego-Superego differentiation appears as the expression of a *genetic* ambiguity according to which it is either possible to describe an Ego structuring itself from, and 'against', the superego, or an Ego endowing itself with a secondary Superego. In his handling of the Superego, Freud is caught in a dialogic dualism of perspectives: on the one hand, the superego is apprehended as the effect of a socio-cultural implantation aiming at the *control* of the individual, with regard to which he finds himself subjected to a dual persecutory and/or eroto-maniacal astringency; on the other, it is described as an acquisition of the Ego following a narcissistic, seductive manoeuvre of the Id on the basis of which it appropriates its cultural heritage. The Ego–superego differentiation is then posed as the location and stake of a process of subjectivation which, by definition, is indefinite. The formulation Freud borrows from Goethe should be more dialectic still: 'What you have inherited from your fathers, if you don't want to be possessed by it, acquire it and make it your own'.[7] One could also say, 'Where the superego was, let the ego be.' But, so that the shadow of the Superego does not fall upon it, the Ego must not seek 'to leap over its shadow'.

At this point, I asked myself what, from a subjective point of view, spurred me to retrace, with you, here in Vienna, Freud's journey to Athens and to analyze his estrangement on the Acropolis. I then recalled the circumstances of my own discovery of the Acropolis. It was in 1946, when I was fourteen, and my family and I were returning from Alexandria to Marseilles after six years of exile due to the war. We took advantage of the stop-over in Piraeus to go and visit the site. My father, a professor of ancient Greek, was our guide, and I recall with shame that, despite our interest in culture, my older brother and I were drawn more to the spectacle of the beautiful Athenian women than to the Parthenon. Since then, happily, I have had the opportunity of approximating the feeling of delight and elevation mentioned by Freud. Retroactively, I found the contrast between our two situations almost comical, but I will not go into the details of my self-analysis here. I will only say that, by returning to the Acropolis with Freud, I vividly felt the nostalgia of the obstacles that he had to surmount in what was for him a veritable conquest. I believe that it is also a matter here of a typical manifestation of the Superego: to the 'too good to be true' corresponds a 'too easy to have any value'.

In the same way, I should say that by setting off again on the traces of his elucidation, I was inhabited by the desire 'to go further than him' on the path of interpretation. And it was my identification with the ideal that he represents that underpinned this ineluctable rivalry. This time, I too had to overcome an impression of the *impermissible*, to disregard a feeling of inferiority which, in my case, of course, was not only a result of my punitive, infantile superego.

But is it not Freud himself who compels us and urges us to take up this indefinitely transgressive step? There is something exciting in the final attempt of the old man to expose the result of a fragment of self-analysis by attributing it, as in 'dream interpretation', a universal significance. It is as though, as he neared the end of his journey, the inventor of psychoanalysis returned to his point of departure; as if he wanted us to recall that it all begins with the method of free association. If Freud's shadow, in the form of a potentially alienating analytic Superego, does not in fact fall on us, it is because what is fundamental in the transmission is due to the fundamental rule. The rule places all attempts at analysis under the sign of a beginning, a discovery; but it truly comes into existence only through the process of subjectivation which gives it meaning.

Addendum: On the Acropolis

If Trieste is the starting point, then Athens is the goal attained, marked by the feeling of estrangement on the Acropolis.[8] The incredulity which in Trieste concerned the desirable project now concerns its realization, which it is going to upset. A sudden thought—an incidental idea—comes to Freud's mind (1936: 241: 'So all this really *does* exist, just as we learnt at school!' Freud describes his inner splitting with precision:[9] a part of his ego 'does not believe its eyes', as if he was seeing something whose *real* existence had always been doubted—and he gives as an illustration of this the Loch Ness Monster; the other part of his ego (the one that had never doubted the existence of Athens was expecting to experience delight and a feeling of elevation) is astonished. By reflecting on his ardent and long-standing desire to travel, and on the belated character of its realization, Freud thus summarizes the meaning of his incidental idea: 'I could really not have imagined it possible that I should ever be granted the sight of Athens with my own eyes' (p. 243). He then closely analyzes the distortion that it reflects. It consists in a double displacement: the present doubt is displaced towards the past as a schoolboy and it no longer concerns his own relationship with Athens, but the very existence of the city. What he had held in doubt during his schooldays was ever seeing Athens with his own eyes. This *legitimized* doubt from school leads Freud to state that the doubt about the existence of Athens well expresses how the perceived reality was put into doubt. But, by clinging to the derealization, I think that Freud dismisses this aspect of surreality that the reference to the Loch Ness Monster seems to suggest. He continues his exposé by keeping to an overview of the range of phenomena touching on the derealization-depersonalization pairing.[10] Once he has noted the complexity of these phenomena and the impossibility of giving a more precise exposé, he retains two aspects of estrangement: it is a matter of a defense mechanism against a threat coming from the external or internal world; and it puts the tie to the past into play, whether the 'ego's store of memories' or 'distressing experiences' (p. 246). He thus proposes a crucial double opposition between outer and inside and pleasure and displeasure.[11]

In a letter to Arnold Zweig, Freud says of his text that it turns on the rogue and the attractive woman: the first promises more than he gives and the second cannot give what she has. This very Freudian humour prompts him 'to go further than the father'. Pertinent research has brought out the symbolic stakes of the spectacle lying before Freud from the heights of the Acropolis.[12] For my part I should like to try to explore closer the difference between the censured desire in Trieste and the upset enjoyment on the Acropolis. Freud tells us nothing about what Athens represented for him during his schooldays; he thus does not tell us anything about the possible role of the Superego in what made him then doubt ever seeing Athens with his own eyes. He therefore seems to repeat in his writings the projection of the Superego described in the malaise in Trieste. And yet, it is significant that he alludes to the 'store of memories' that the estrangement depends on. Since we are aware of what the power of his imagination and the intensity of his identification with great conquerors—Alexander, Hannibal—were, we might think that, in his reveries, it sometimes occurred to him that he *was* Alexander mounting the Acropolis in order to *take possession* of it.[13] There were moments when Athens confused a voyage in space with a voyage in time. And repression had to work, the reality principle had to impose its law, so that the voyage to Athens could only be envisaged as an accessible or inaccessible reality. I presume that the acquisition of academic knowledge, under the superego authority of his school masters, contributed to the sublimatory transposition of the over-cathected reveries. The identification with the archeologist superceded that of Alexander.[14] We are aware of the complexity of what is hanging in the balance in the structuring of the Ego-Superego space regarding the identificatory modifications leading to an Ego-Ideal.

The satisfaction the forty-eight-year old traveler was hoping for, was expecting—the delight and elevation—is complex. It implies the delicate conjunction, but only subjectively satisfying, between his informed contemplation of the site and the actualization of his private imagination attached to the past of Greek antiquity. The estrangement signs the partial failure, at least, of this conjunction, the exact nature is clarified by certain indications in Freud's text. The entire experience, he says, is marked by a certain atmosphere of fear that explains the silence of the two brothers and illustrates, with a persecutory tonality, the Superego's hostility projected onto the atmosphere. But Freud also indirectly alludes to the precariousness of repression, which suggests an irruptive actualization of the subjective *treasure*. In referring to 'The Uncanny',[15] I suggest that the threat did not concern the return of repressed infantile desire but rather that of 'modes of functioning one had thought overcome'. The heroic reveries evoked above might correspond to these modes of thought: during his schooldays, faced with a mixture of a constraining reality and an interdicting superego, the young Sigmund did not want to believe, *in his Unconscious*, in the inexistence of the Athens of his dreams: he was dubious as to one part of what he had learned, namely, that there existed nothing but ruins in Athens.[16] I thus imagine that the seductive solicitation of the site aroused in him, with the nostalgia for a lost Athens, the temptation of an animistic regression, of a self-hypnotic state. One may then measure the defensive complexity of the estrangement if the Ego must oscillate between the derealization tied to the Superego's reproach and the surreality tied to the irruptive proximity of the id-impulses. The incredulity refers to three intertwined doubts: the old rational doubt relative to objective obstacles, the doubt stemming from the repression of Oedipal desire, and the paradoxical doubt tied to the refusal to give up omnipotence whose ineluctability is illustrated by the reduction of ancient Athens to ruins. To these contradictory movements are added the possibility that Freud had waited too long for the trip and that, as the circumstances would have it, opportunity makes a thief: it thus hardly assumes the grandiosity which, Freud emphasizes, colours the voyage of the adolescent. I thus imagine a Freud pulled between contradictory feelings with, possibly, a shade of disappointment despite the strong impression the Parthenon makes on him. What he is missing, at the moment he confronts the object of his old desire, is, undoubtedly, the feeling of the *effectiveness* of reality. As C. and S. Botella (2006) have emphasized, this feeling is not at all tied to perceptive reality alone, since it may accompany, for instance, the memory of a dream. The verbal formulation, in its defensive function, involves the recollecting which places the subject back again in time, barring the way to possible retrogressive functioning.

Notes

1. Translated by Steven Jaron, and revised for this edition.
2. Translator's note: The SE renders the German *'unerlaubt'* as 'forbidden'. The author feels Laplanche rightfully avoids using the term *'interdit'* (forbidden), preferring *'non-permis'* (not permitted or unauthorized).
3. And, of course, the analytic treatment must be thought of as a journey, an odyssey.

4. Which, in function of a logic of perversion, may lead to a reversal whereby what is forbidden gives birth to desire. This is why it seems important to take into account the nuance implied by Freud's German term *'unerlaubt'*, translated by Laplanche by *'non-permis'*. What is at stake is the possibility of going beyond the alternative 'forbidden-permitted' involved in the logic of infantile dependence in order to accede to a freedom which is nonetheless always conflictual.

5. Though Alexander is a merchant like the father, the transgression is not made any easier.

6. At the time he was writing his letter to Romain Rolland, Freud was working on his *Moses*, whose composition and publication, we know, posed a great deal of problems.

7. The SE translation reads: 'What thou hast inherited from thy fathers, acquire it to make it thine' (SE 13, p. 158).

8. In truth, the brief stay in Athens was entirely marked by a certain malaise tied, it seems, to the severity of the conflict with Fliess. Freud was prey to an impressive invasion of a number of obsessions related to *strange* coincidences in reality. (Cf. *op. cit.*)

9. The existence of this split poses the difficult question of the relationship between the ego-superego *split* and the 'splitting of the ego in the process of defense'. One should note that the inner discourse is not addressed to the other part of the ego, which conjures up a reduplication of the splitting.

10. I will return to the hypothesis, mentioned in passing, according to which at the time of his schooling Freud would not have believed in the existence of Athens *in his unconscious*. Having described the complementarity between derealization and depersonalization, concerning their value as defenses, he allusively evokes the occasional hallucinations of healthy individuals: *déjà vu* (evidence of an animistic life prior to the ego), dual consciousness and the split personality.

11. The first is related rather to derealization and the second, to depersonalization. The superego is the intermediary between the outer and the inner.

12. Cf. *op. cit.* The accent is most often placed on the register of the maternal object. On another register, it has been highlighted that behind the Parthenon is silhouetted the Temple of Jerusalem.

13. We know that as an adolescent Freud kept his diary in ancient Greek. Jones relates that during the voyage to Athens, he believed he could communicate with his taxi driver in this language. Such a

lack of understanding of temporal distance doubtlessly illustrates a telescoping of the various levels of time in his psyche.

14. Like the Oedipal child who, in his family romance, denies the primitive scene and turns himself a hero, which gives way to the ambitious son placed in the order of generations and equipped with an ego-ideal.
15. In this essay Freud distinguishes between two modes of the feeling of strangeness. The first is not threatening to the ego, as it is a matter of the representational return of repressed infantile desire (incest, castration); the second puts the functioning of the ego into question, as it concerns modes of omnipotent animistic thought (often relative to death and the inanimate) which, one would have believed, had been overcome.
16. I am echoing here the somewhat strange formulation of Freud, mentioned above, which makes him write that the profound hypothesis which he does not believe in the existence of Athens *in his unconscious* is 'easier to assert than to prove'.

References

Botella, C. and S. (2006). 'Pour une métapsychologie de la remémoration'. In André Green (*dir*), *Les voies nouvelles de la thérapeutique psychanalytique. Le dedans et le dehors*. Paris: Presses Universitaires de France, pp. 709–732.

Donnet, J.-L. (1995). Surmoi (1) Le concept freudien et la règle fondamentale. Monographies de la *Revue Française de Psychanalyse* Paris: Presses Universitaires de France.

Freud, S. (1912–1913). *Totem and Taboo. SE, 13*: 1–161.

Freud, S. (1921). *Group Psychology and the Analysis of the Ego. SE, 18*: 67–143.

Freud, S. (1923). *The Ego and the Id. SE, 19*: 3–63.

Freud, S. (1924). 'The Economic Problem of Masochism'. *SE, 19*: 155–170.

Freud, S. (1936). 'A Disturbance of Memory on the Acropolis'. *SE, 22*: 239–248.

CHAPTER EIGHT

Work of culture and superego

(I) I would like to take up certain crucial issues in Freud's *Civilization and its Discontents* (1930), a text that is more topical than ever.

Freud contends in this text that the cultural process, like the individual process, is of an instinctual and vital nature—that is to say, determined *in the last resort* by the conflictual interplay of the drives. The work of culture is envisaged there in terms of the essential link connecting the notion of psychic work with the instinctual economy. I will try to reconstruct what was at stake for Freud in the instinctual drive transformations that it implies. The Superego is designated by Freud in *The Future of an Illusion* (1927) as the most patent manifestation of psychical acquisitions linked to the work of culture; it is also the most precious indication of the value of the drive transformations obtained.

Both processes are articulated with each other by means of the metaphor of a planet which revolves at once around its own axis and around the sun. The difference of their aim explains their relative antagonism. Freud (1930, p. 140) writes: 'In the developmental process of the individual, the programme of the pleasure principle, which consists in finding the satisfaction of happiness, is retained as the main aim. Integration in, or adaptation to, a human community appears as a scarcely avoidable condition ... But in the process of civilization things are different. Here by far the most important thing is the aim of creating a unity out of the individual human beings ... It almost seems as if the creation of a great human community would be most successful if no attention had to be paid to the happiness of the individual.'

The work of culture can only reflect this obviously variable antagonism. An essential reference is that of the group structure identified in *Group Psychology and the Analysis of the Ego* (1921): the bond of identification which welds individuals together is assured by sharing the Ideal Superego; so there is no gap here between the individual and the group.

By postulating in *Civilization and its Discontents* the existence of a cultural Superego, distinct from the individual Superego, Freud recognizes the potential gap between them. The cultural Superego is a vehicle of the long temporality of the species, marked by the historical vicissitudess of a culture. The individual Superego appears, in one sense, to be its counterpart when, according to Freud's indications, it is formed in the image of the parents' Superego, which suggests a pure transgenerational repetition. But in fact it is marked by the diversity of individual dispositions and the historical vicissitudes of childhood.

The essential link between the two Superegos proceeds from the equivalence between the childhood of humanity and the childhood of each individual. Just as each individual development supposes a gap between child and parent (or educator), so the cultural process implies a gap between the masses and cultural heroes who incarnate and remodel the collective Superego. We cannot know if the cultural hero derives his necessity from the transference of the father of childhood or from the phylogenetic heritage; nor can we know if the father derives his sacred character from infantile distress or from the transference of the primal father. Freud does not exclude the possibility that radically different cultural and educative conditions may reduce the gap between the leaders and the led; but it is very clear that the work of culture finds in the individual process a more accessible and more diversified potential for evolution. The gap between the Ego and the Superego, by virtue of its very conflictuality, is a vehicle of effects of subjectivation which, of course, are also a function of the cultural Superego of the time.[1] The work of the differentiation between Ego and Superego underlies analytic work.

(II) By removing us *ever further* from the conditions of life of our ancestors,[2] the process of civilization also leads us away from their direct, quasi-animal instinctual satisfactions. The structuring of the psyche goes hand in hand with the 'psychization' of the instinctual drives, even though the force of their pressure never loses its power to overwhelm traumatically the psychical apparatus. This is why Freud, as a clinician, strives to evaluate the economy of the instinctual drive transformations, their *cost*, their viability, their stability and their reversibility. He measures the efficacy of the symbolic function. Because the first element of the work of culture is frustration, he always wonders if culture compensates man sufficiently for the renunciations and sacrifices that it imposes on him. He thus refuses to idealise the work of culture, a marked characteristic of which is self-idealisation. In the last analysis, he considers that 'we owe to that process the best of what we have become as well as a good part of what we suffer from (1933, p. 214).

The sexual drives

The sexual drives offer the best illustration of what is at stake in this work. The individual process has revealed their ubiquity and their structural link with the pleasure principle. At the phylogenetic level, it is based on the mutation which, in particular, has made it lose the periodicity of rut.[3] The work of culture uses both the mobility and the fixability of the libido. Its constant pressure seems to find an extension in the imperishability of unconscious wishes. The sexual drive proves itself capable of displacing indefinitely its aims by desexualising them, and of creating-investing new objects, while idealising them. Hence the importance of the inhibition of aims, of the multiple forms of love. *Ananke* would not have succeeded in obtaining the collaboration of men for the shared aims of self-preservation without the sublimated homosexual love that underlies social relations.

Each stage of the process of civilization corresponds to the demand for a new form of relationship and a new distribution of investments, giving rise to an intra-erotic conflictuality which remains viable in spite of the limitations imposed on sexual pleasure, for example, by the prohibition of incest. The opposition between narcissism and object-cathexes is a general model, identifiable in each individual, but also at each level of group functioning (narcissism of small differences). However, the issue of identification complicates the question of investments. Freud describes primary identification as a primitive oral instinctual mode and the prohibition against cannibalism as the most deeply inscribed prohibition of all. In the light of this fundamental ambivalence, identification is also described as a mimetic relationship, at a distance, which can acquire a counter or even anti-instinctual dimension.

The question of sublimation and of the over-investment of higher psychic activities constitutes a crucial issue at stake in the work of culture.

Sublimation is defined as a displacement of the aim of the drive. Freud sometimes seems tempted to describe it as a process which avoids repression, affords complete satisfaction, and culminates in a realization in line with the ideals of culture. In its generalized version (cf. its role in working life), it would then be a joker of the work of culture, by doing away with the very notion of compensation. But Freud's position remains ambiguous and he has doubts in particular about the scope of the sublimatory solution.

Above all, it seems to me, the question of sublimation is linked with the question of the over-investment of the higher psychical activities. To be sure, this hypercathexis underlies, owing to the epistemophilic displacement of the libido, the formidable deployment of the world of representation, signs, and language, utilizing the imaginary and symbolic capacities of the human brain. If this immense work of culture opens out on to the progress of reason, it also opens out on to the madness, credulousness, and suggestibility of man: *homo sapiens-demens* (Edgar Morin).

From the point of view of instinctual drive activity, the *hyper-cathexis* is an excess: it corresponds globally to a displacement from below to above, towards that which is elevated, pure and sublime. For Freud, the sublime is a mode of experiencing pleasure, before serving as a support for a value judgement. In *Leonardo da Vinci* (1910) he pointed out that originally the genitals were the pride and hope of man, signifying voluptuousness and procreation, and were venerated as such. The work of culture transfers the divine towards heaven and tends to give value to desexualisation. Does this not result, then, in feelings of shame, and even disgust for the genitals, in the depreciation of sexuality? This raises the question of finding the right narcissistic balance between pride and humility, if the work of culture indeed contains this tendency to decorporealize man by cutting him off from his animality ... from his childhood. This tendency is also a consequence of the repression of anality—linked perhaps to the upright, erect position—in favour of the visual. Freud underlines the importance of the collective reactive formations of anality in what defines culture: the taste for order and cleanliness and, to some extent, the taste for beauty. In short, the hypercathexis of higher psychical activities allows for the transition from sublimation as a mere displacement of aim to the sublimation of aims.

It is also worth pointing out that this hypercathexis cannot easily be distinguished from a sexualization of thought processes. For Freud, the animistic mode of thinking is not only a spontaneous projective anthropomorphic manifestation; it is a way of exerting influence on nature just as we have learnt to exert influence on the higher beings on whom we depend.

In the obsessional neurosis of humanity, the equivalent of infantile neurosis, the magic power of thought and words on beings and things is the projective displacement of the actual power exerted by wishes on thought. In certain respects, the same omnipotence underlies the Superego's claim to legislate for psychic reality, without taking the obstacles into account; for it is the reversal of the drive force which underlies this claim. The hypercathexis of the higher psychic activities supports the work of symbolization which binds the violence of the drives psychically; but it also nourishes the violence of conflicts of opinion: the combat continues in the realm of ideas with increased violence.

The introduction of the death drive modified the situation.

In *Totem and Taboo* (1912–13), the inaugural murderous aggression was a reactive act, motivated by the wish to take possession of the women and power; it was made possible by the union of the brothers as a result of ambivalence about the return of love, the symbolic act of exogamy, and the totemic meal guaranteeing the collective sharing of real guilt: in short, it was a passionate murder, under *the aegis of Eros*.

If aggression is an *innate* drive, the first task of the work of culture becomes its repression through internalization, thus its reversal against the Ego: unconscious guilt is this internal aggression of the Superego against the Ego, the paradoxical feature of which is that it is nourished by unaccomplished acts. After *Totem and Taboo*, it was easier to commit a murder than to erase the trace of it. After *Civilization and its Discontents,* it seems easier to renounce the idea of committing a murder than to erase the trace of this renunciation. Lacan would draw from this the recommendation 'not to give way on one's desire'.

Guilt always finds its principal origin in love: love for the other, and love of the other, which sustain the organization, thanks to the uniting function of the object, of a sufficiently masochistic pleasure principle. But the death drive gives the cultural or individual Super-ego its predilection for cruelty, conferring on its prescriptions their tyrannical and unreal character.

The cultural process thus seems to be woven by the tragic confrontation of the two irreconcilable forces of Eros and the death drive. Owing to its vital function of fusion or union, the work of culture operates very closely with the compulsion to repeat. It seems to be condemned to an indefinitely recurrent task, a perpetual attempt. But the permanent danger of barbaric regression outwits the tendency of a desexualized Eros to mass unification. It is no longer Eros, Freud says, which serves the civilizing process, but the contrary, and for a more obscure purpose.

The work of culture is infiltrated by an ineluctable hostility with regard to culture itself—hostility arising from the failures of culture, notably from the external, yet unavoidable manifestations of aggression, but also primary hostility linked to the frustration of aggression and to the unease of guilt. This double register of hostility means that it is difficult to discern within progressive socio-cultural movements between what may be regarded as just revolt and what amounts to a radical rejection of the constraints of culture. Freud writes that he himself had denied for a long time the existence of a death drive. He thus suggests that hostility against culture—identifiable in many religious themes—seems to have to be denied, as does the immemorial failure of culture in the domain of human relations. Freudian rationality would like this denial to be lifted so that the truthful knowledge of psychical reality might make action possible, as is the case with the forces of nature. But can this denial really be lifted? Is it not constitutive of a work of culture which, if it is to begin to reject what is barbarian, needs the outsider representing anti-culture? The triad denial-splitting-projection and the pair idealization-persecution are the primitive foundations of the psyche, and remain those which operate in the superego functioning of the group mind. The work of culture rests first of all on a judgement of attribution, which, as Freud shows in his article on 'Negation' (1925), is inherent to the drive conflict and precedes, by definition, the judgement of existence. One may well ask if the work of culture is not based structurally on a judgement of attribution presented as a judgement of value.

At the end of *Civilization and its Discontents*, Freud (1930, p. 145) in fact asserts that the only thing he knows for certain is that 'man's judgements of value follow directly his wishes for happiness—that accordingly, they are an attempt to support his illusions with arguments.' He was thereby acknowledging not only the immense field of rationalization, but also the structural implication of illusion in the work of culture.

Superego and work of culture

The distinctive ambiguities of the work of culture can be found in the agency of the Superego.

There is a current in Freudian thought which tends to regard the Superego as an implantation in psychic space of a significant part of the external world, as a forced encounter between the Id and reality, from which the Ego will have to draw inspiration. The Superego appears as a core of the Ego, dominating it to the extent that it has internalized relations of vital dependency between the individual and his group, as well as between the child and his parents. The danger of a loss of love and of counter-aggression presides over this *inculcation* in such a way that for the Ego, the Superego will remain the vector of a reality of the other that is marked by a double constraint: persecutory and erotomaniac.

This notion of the Superego as a colony implanted by culture to control the individual stands in contrast with another which sees the establishment of the Superego as a narcissistic manoeuvre of the Ego, and the first phase of a subjectivizing appropriation: 'What thou hast inherited from thy fathers, acquire it to make it thine' (Goethe). The work of differentiating the Ego and Superego, and the identificatory revisions (symbolic identifications) which lead to the post-oedipal normativization and to the function of the Ideal will then be described.

It may be safely assumed, however, that the development of the Superego towards symbolic impersonalisation cannot go as far as the complete desexualization of the figures of destiny evoked by Freud.

Because the Superego is an agency that is as irreducible to the Ego as the Id, it constitutes a structural reserve of illusion: it perpetuates something of the relation big/little which sustains the wish to be big, but also the wish to remain or to become little again.

In this respect, humour, a theme to which Freud returns in 1927, is evidence of a rare but exemplary achievement of the work of culture, turning even the most unfavourable circumstances into an occasion for sublime enjoyment. To this end, the Ego decathects itself in favour of the Superego to which it restores reality-testing by way of consolation: a psychical play of illusion that rests on the simultaneous recognition and denial of reality.

Analytic work and work of culture?

1. Freud sometimes refers to analysis as a post-education. If education corresponds to the work of culture in the individual process, the expression makes it clear that the analytic work that extends it is neither an equivalent nor a substitute. From a strictly analytic point of view, a sufficiently successful education would be one that permits the subject to become an analysand. The analytic work occurs retrospectively.[4]

   We can also say that analytic work postulates, as one of its axes, an agency in order to analyze the superego and to autonomize the ego. A paradox of the fundamental rule is that the transgressive activity that it proposes only assumes meaning in relation to the consistency of the Ego-Superego conflict that it induces. The fruitful ambiguity of the analytic situation is to promote the transferential illusion in order to permit a more civilizing disillusionment, while preserving the capacity for transference.

   Furthermore, through the means that it utilizes, and thus valorizes, analytic work implies a certain hypercathexis of the higher psychical activities that is indispensable for the enactment of the unconscious. The cost in unpleasure of the method has to be compensated for by a quota of sublimatory, epistemophilic and aesthetic enjoyment. However, the purpose of analytic treatment is not sublimation, but only the relative harmonization of a drive equation that is always singular.

What is important in the *so es war,* and the asymptotic outcome that it implies, is not so much the mastery of the drives, which could remain under the sway of the Superego, as the modification of the relations Ego-Superego and the introjection of the drives into the Ego.

2. How should analytic work be situated in relation to the interference between the individual and cultural processes—interference in which both complementarity and antagonism are manifested?

What is at stake here can be identified in the question of cure *as an additional benefit.* In an immediate way, this character of additional benefit refers to the necessary functional autonomy of the method. The method postulates, however, that its activation will have beneficial effects in the patient's life, but indirect, mediate effects that can be grouped together under the term of cure as soon as, beyond the improvement of symptoms, they refer to a state of positive psychic health, for example, the freedom to love and work. If this postulate is found wanting, the method has to find a remedy by constructing its condition of possibility: there is no such thing as pure psychoanalysis. A paradox of the psychoanalyst's responsibility is that these effects of the analytic process escape him to a large extent and depend on extrinsic factors that are often contingent. But they are none the less the specific consequence of the psychic transformations inherent to the activation of the method (lifting of repression, working through of resistances).

By contending that cure is not an additional benefit, Nathalie Zaltzmann (1998) is not only asserting that psychic transformations concern the field of intersubjective relations. She contends that, by modifying the instinctual base of the reality-principle, analytic work includes structurally everything that is connected with relations with others. In order to delimit clearly my disagreement, I want first to confirm that the effects of analytic work cannot fail to manifest themselves in the subject's object-relations. It is simply a question of knowing to what extent these effects are *analytic.*

In a good many cases, as the experience of child and adolescent psychoanalysis regularly shows, the analytic function undoubtedly seems to radiate on to the whole family system, for example.

There are thus grounds for evoking the continuation of personal analytic work in a dynamic of elaborative inter-subjectivization. Symmetrically, the group psychoanalytic approach has a specific effect on the individual psyche.

When psychoanalytic work has such influence, it can be said that it confers on the antagonism of several individual processes or, more generally, the individual process and the collective process, a positive value of complementarity. We can then consider that, in this ideal register, isomorphism exists between analytic work and the work of culture.

But it scarcely seems possible to generalize this model. The repercussions of analytic work on the subject's environment are not necessarily psychoanalytic, and do not necessarily work towards an intersubjective elaboration that is conflictual but reciprocally beneficial. The analysed subject often finds himself obliged to impose decisions which conform with his new personal equation, or to renounce doing so for various reasons, ethical or realistic. We can see, then, to what extent analytic work is centred on the programme of the individual process, and that it seems very difficult to extrapolate from the specific metapsychology of the session towards the field of intersubjective or institutional relations. In the analytic situation, the desire of the other makes itself present through the prism of the transference, and it seems useful, even if the structuring of the subject implies the other, to maintain the distinction between the intrapsychic and the inter-psychic. The example of analytic institutions illustrates sufficiently the non-coincidence between the intra-analytic and the inter-analytic. Even if it is not certain that analytic institutions are worse than others, it is clear that personal analytic work often seems to exacerbate the antagonism between the individual process and the group process.

Psychoanalytic cure is the result of the conjunction-disjunction of specific transformations and effects whose manifestation is aleatory and contingent.

As for the relations between analytic work and work of culture, I think it is inevitable that they sometimes emphasize their isomorphy, and sometimes their heteromorphy. They need to be described in terms of the gap and the complex interferences between the respective evolutional potentialities of the individual Superego and the cultural Superego. Basically one would find at the heart of the relations between the subject and the group the problem of sublimation: sublimatory realization is not defined by its conformity with pre-established cultural demands, but as an occasional and creative resolution of the structural antagonism between the individual process and the cultural process.

3. There was a lot of discussion in the seventies (cf. Freudo-Marxism, Marcuse) about the relations between analytic work and individual/group relations. I just want to draw attention here to the socio-cultural conditioning of analytic practice. This practice needs the cultural Superego and its Ideals to guarantee it the minimal support of respecting private space and freedom of thought. In exchange, it is postulated that the psychic transformations inherent to the psychoanalytic project are not incompatible with the said Ideals. The psychoanalytic adventure is certainly transgressive, but it nonetheless hopes that the cultural Superego will valorize this transgression.

However, the effect of Psychoanalysis on Culture is very difficult to evaluate. There is no doubt that the diffusion of psychoanalytic knowledge has marked the field of culture, and in particular the field of education. But after a century, is not the prevalent impression one of misunderstanding? Freud expresses irritation in *Civilization and its Discontents* at how the cultural hero he has become is required to be prophet, a consoler, someone who has the answers. But can the cultural effect of psychoanalysis be psychoanalytic if speaking *about psychoanalysis* means being outside psychoanalysis? The effect of psychoanalysis on culture generally remains caught in an ideal Superego register, whether it is a case of submitting to it or of refusing to do so. There is indeed something irreplaceable in the actual practice of analytic work: only the structured situation and the analysis of the transference make it possible to really work through the resistance of the Superego. It could even be suggested that all analytic work should potentially make a cultural hero of the subject, but would not such a prescription illustrate the paradox of the Ideal Superego?

Notes

1. In *The Future of an Illusion*, Freud shows clearly how it is necessary to suspend the question of the economic interests which apparently dominate the process of civilization in order to gain access to the psychological factors which are *ultimately* decisive: the instinctual drive economy and its principles of functioning.
2. The corresponding passage in the SE (1930, 89) reads : 'We shall therefore content ourselves with saying once more that the word 'civilization' describes the whole sum of the achievements and the regulations which distinguish our lives from those of our animal ancestors ...'. The French translation uses the verb *s éloigner* rather than 'distinguish', which is more in line with the notion of cultural process that Freud has just evoked.
3. To this could be added the organic repression of smell; ultimately, the sexual drives have become incapable of full satisfaction.
4. In child psychoanalysis, the concomitance of the educative and the analytic was a crucial issue between Anna Freud and Melanie Klein.

References

Freud, S. (1910). *Leonard da Vinci and a Memory of his Childhood. SE, 11*: 57–137.

Freud, S. (1912–1913). *Totem and Taboo. SE, 13*: 1–161.

Freud, S. (1921). *Group Psychology and the Analysis of the Ego. SE, 18*: 65–143.

Freud, S. (1925). *Negation. SE, 19*: 233–239.

Freud, S. (1927). *The Future of an Illusion. SE, 21*: 1–56.

Freud, S. (1930). *Civilization and its Discontents. SE, 21*: 59–145.

Zaltzman, N. (1998). *De la guérison psychanalytique.* Paris : Presses Universitaires de France.

CHAPTER NINE

A child is being talked about[1]

(I) During an analysis, it is not uncommon for a scene from the distant or not so distant past, with the privileged value of a screen-memory, to reappear, which the patient might resume as follows: 'They were speaking about me.'

'They' may refer to two or three people, family members, friends or teachers; typically, of course, it is the parental couple. It is the tone and theme of the exchange overheard which are initially striking, colouring the evocation: something said in confidence, a discussion or dispute, praise or criticism, a presumption, worry or project; each of these registers will have awakened diverse but well-defined feelings. Initially, then, it is the significance of the words heard and their affective resonance which give the memory its value; they nourish the associative chains and support the work of interpretation.

(II) Sometimes, however, the content of the conversation escapes the patient, remains uncertain or seems to have been repressed; at other times, it is the very identity of the one who was being talked about that is in doubt. Perhaps it was someone else, a sibling, for example. And this doubt then seems to become the central issue. It is even conceivable that the scene occurred in the child's presence, if it was assumed that he or she could not understand the dialogue—which may even have taken place in a foreign language.

Then, naturally, the meaning of the words no longer counts. What is immediately noticeable—but constitutes a second phase in all cases—is the nature of the fantasy that the screen memory depicts. The scene runs as follows: the subject heard himself being referred to by his first name, or its diminutive, when in fact he was not the one being spoken to; or alternatively, he thought he recognized himself in the words 'that child ...', 'your son ...', 'our daughter ...'; in a more exemplary manner, his/her presence was reduced to a 'he' or 'she' in the dialogue. In short, the child was the *object* of an enunciation.

Thus condensed, it may be that the scene only aroused in the subject a sense of hungry and vaguely guilty curiosity (should I have turned a deaf ear?). But sometimes the memory remains animated by a violent affect containing a mixture of pleasure and shame.

(III) In this second phase of its analysis, the screen-memory proves to be the actualisation of a fundamental question whose answer, as we know, is always concealed: 'Who am I, who am I for them?' Beyond the diversity of the themes, the situation seems to put the subject in a position to surprise the real desire of the other. If I am being talked about, in my absence, I will obviously be able to understand what I represent for them, which is always *concealed* from me when they know I am present, since what they say can always be suspected of yielding to my demand (do you love me?) or of rejecting it.

But in the fleeting moment when the child was listening very closely to what was being said, he may have got a glimpse of the trap which might reduce him to being nothing more than that, and of the essential and fatal transgression which would condemn him to coincide with this other of himself, and to meet up with his double in the mirror of others. This moment bears witness to the burning upheaval comprised of pleasure and shame.

As if to circumscribe the fantasy and to immobilise the dizziness that it arouses, the scene is reduced to the skeleton of a nomination which nonetheless preserves its suspense. In such a way, in fact, that the memory transformed into a screen-memory has become the enactment of a simultaneous question and a response which are self-sufficient: since they are talking about me, it means that I am the object of their thoughts, love or concern. My absence does not make me disappear; it does not abolish my presence. I remain between my parents to unite and separate them: being the link between them forms the bridge between presence and absence.

(IV) 'They are talking about me' is to be interpreted first, then, in the light of the theme, and then in the light of the structure of the fantasy.

But, as we have just seen, this realization of the fantasy also conceals within it, as its condition of possibility, the subject's relation to language. If presence and absence are interchangeable, the designating operator must play its role. This operator is exemplarily the pronoun 'he'. If he is to be present in his absence, present by his absence, the child must be able to recognize himself in this 'he', and to tolerate this dispossession implied by an objectification which reduces him, fleetingly, to the signifier itself of the 'anonymous'. In the register of affect, the memory combines the exquisite exasperation of the sense of subjectivity and the anguished threat of annihilation. This objectification which makes him self-divided, non-identical with himself, is linked to the eventual emergence of the beginnings of a state of depersonalisation in which the impression of the unreality of oneself and that of too much reality are mixed. After a moment of impotent revolt, and even of quasi-despair, this depersonalisation resolves itself into a slightly miraculous and yet strangely familiar sense of fatality.

(V) I shall refer here to the inspired article by Luce Irigaray (1966), 'Communication linguistique et communication spéculaire'. The author compares the body of language and the imaginary body in an attempt to articulate the reciprocity of their integration. She sets out to describe a *mirroring* in language which would be the equivalent or the corollary of the mirror stage. The unity of the body which is 'imaginarised' in the Ego (in the Lacanian sense) has as its counterpart the unity of the signifier 'so-and-so'. Luce Irigaray proposes a strictly linguistic formulation of this fruitful moment which corresponds to what seemed to me to constitute the interpretive matrix of the screen-memory. The first phases of communication through language, as rich as they may be, and even before the advent of the 'I' and the 'you' in relation to the speech of a third party, only open the way, she writes, to a dialogue without permutation or retroversion.

It is because, and when the parents communicate together, because the I becomes you, and the you becomes I, that they become (you and I) relations and no longer terms. And this decisive moment is linked to the fact that the child has been a 'he', in other words, an empty space, an empty form vouching for the structure of exchange, a negation which permits the structure to exist as such; a moment when the child is excluded from communication while at the same time being integrated with it, and which presupposes the experience of a first death, the experience of nothingness, a support of identification. It is a structuring moment when the *infans* encounters a key point in the structure of communication and he can only appropriate it, make it his own, by first being an object.

Focusing primarily on the question of liberating oneself from linguistic castration, Luce Irigaray is led to postulate that the castrator is the structure of communication itself. Perhaps the requirement of closing the structure marks the limit of a perspective which nonetheless had as its aim the *reciprocal* integration of language and the body; it is true that the body referred to is that of the specular image.

The screen-memory, which was my starting-point, opens out onto the historicity of the subject. I am not thinking of the stages that mark the gradual access of the *infans* to the handling of language and symbolic thought; for the psychic representation, *a child is being talked about*, comprises the *discontinuity* introduced by symbolic castration, the loss that it implies, and the power that proceeds from it; it enacts the structure of the *après-coup* itself, since it signifies a before and an after, and henceforth it is with words that the subject will seek to account for this transition. The uncanniness of lived experience is linked to the anticipated return of an outdated mode of thinking, to the unthinkable possibility of a lifting of primary repression.

Historicity is directly present in the screen-memory insofar as it not *only refers to the spoken subject but also to the historicised* subject. To be the object of an enunciation is above all to become the object of history. The subject finds he is faced here with a story—a prehistory Freud says—which precedes him, and in relation to which he is *obliged* to situate himself.

One can recognize here the problematic—described by Piera Aulagnier—concerning the identifying statements of the speech-bearer and the identificatory project of the I (*Je*). The screen-memory thus marks the emergence of the apprentice historian; the narrator hero must play with his *spoken shadow*.[2]

(VI) In this register, the screen-memory may constitute a marker in the crucial problematic of the treatment, namely, that of the relations of interpretation-construction with material and historical realities. For Freud, as we know, this issue was first centred on the reality of the repressed memory which returns. In 'Constructions in Analysis' (1937), he nonetheless came to realise that in the absence of such a return a construction can lead to an assured conviction. In his book *La Construction de l'espace analytique*,[3] Serge Viderman (1971) argues in favour of the idea of the ultimately radically *creative* character of speech in the session. The liveliness of the discussions aroused by his book underline the pertinence of the question.

It seems to me that the analysis of the screen-memory throws some useful light on this debate, by emphasizing the genitico-structural conditions underlying the very possibility of a total conviction arising from a construction of the psychoanalyst.

In the analytic situation, as in the scene of the screen-memory, a major issue is the subject's relation with a *story told* which can become his own and be subjectivized, that is, which transcends the influence characteristic of suggestion. A few remarks will suffice to draw out the differences that can be observed clinically.

- Some patients, especially at the beginning of analysis, find it quite natural to go and question their ascendants in order to compare the accounts given of events of their past with their own memories. In those cases where the process gets underway, the radically intimate and subjective dimension of their activity of remembering and its communication in the transference result in this comparison losing all its meaning.
- For a certain number of patients, for whom the question of a denied family secret is actualised, it is, on the contrary, analytic elaboration that leads them to open an inquiry in reality.
- An interesting scenario here is that of patients for whom, throughout the analysis, the distinction between their own lived memories and family narratives concerning them remains a permanent issue of concern, requiring their vigilance. The experience of such narratives is marked by feelings of embarrassment, of constraint, and is even felt to be a threat to identity; it is reminiscent of the

unpleasant, anxiety-producing aspect of the memory of the scene: *They are talking about me.*

It seems, on the contrary, that the effacement, or at least relativization of the distinction between memory proper and related memory constitutes a positive indication of the development of the process. It is the mark of a harmonious conjunction between the reality-testing of the Ego that of the reliability of the discourse and its symbolic markers. We can postulate that the suspension of their disjunction corresponds to the fact that the experience of the transference is lived in a transitional mode. It is clear that its possibility is to a large extent the product and the reflection of a story: every child has encountered the duality between direct experiences and words heard. The suppleness of their articulation owes much to a sufficient degree of coherence, to the loving quality of the utterances of the speech-bearer, or more profoundly of the parental couple.

A paradox of the analytic situation is that it is precisely with subjects for whom this linguistic environment has been deficient that the problem of a massive infantile amnesia is posed most acutely and thus of the conviction arising from construction. With these subjects the transferential scene is often burdened by the suspicion which saps the interpretive function itself, insofar as it repeats the threat of alienation of the first identifying statements.

In other words, the patient's capacity to allow a construction to work in his mind can become a key issue in the process. It seems to me that this throws light on the ambiguity with which Serge Viderman, while emphasizing the creative dimension of *analytic story*, nonetheless continues to insist with Freud on the importance of the memory: the stratum of the remembered is the necessary support whereby the exploration of the transference creates-finds a new story; so for the child who is spoken about in the sessions, the question of knowing if he *actually* existed can be suspended.

(VII) To conclude, I want to raise the question of the links that exist or that need to be built between the screen-memory and the Freudian *primal scene*, as lived experience and as primal phantasy.

The memory of the primal scene is typically presented as being constituted of perceptual, visual (kinaesthetic), auditory (noises, groans, moans, words), and olfactory leftovers. These traces relate to the confused apprehension of a parental coupling in which the perceptual incompleteness is bound up with the unrepresentable. The consequence of this is usually a traumatic experience linked with the irruption of an uncontrollable quantity of instinctual excitation. This explains the frequency of a fixation of an image that, initially, does not make any sense. The second elaborative phase is only accessible through the sufficiently regressive context of the session, and, for Freud, with the identificatory support of the primal phantasy.

In the course of an analytic process, the memory of the primal scene, by being put into words, can come to signify for the subject his own origin. Such an elaboration allows him to reconcile himself with the sexual and often *shameful* crudeness of this origin, to accept his exclusion by recognizing that he owes it his life, and even by making a gift of absence, which contributes to the payment of his debt.

The screen memory can be linked up all the more easily with the primal scene in that it combines within itself the register of the animal on the watch in relation to the instinctual body and the register of an origin symbolized by the parental discourse. The passivation— being the object of a statement—repeats that of the perceptual and instinctual invasion.

The underlying issue at stake is still the need for sufficient complementarity between on the one hand the maternal care that will assure the organisation of the auto-erotic body, and, on the other, the identifying statements that will assure the symbolic organization and the Ideal Superego function. Thanks to the regressive transferential actualization, to the force of act that it confers on speech, there is a great proximity between the primal scene and the screen-memory, between the reality of things and the reality of words. *A child is being talked about* is then the equivalent of *We are making a child.*

The screen-memory can, however, sometimes become the object of a defensive fetishization whereby the words heard, excluding the issue of instinctual introjection, may be said to commemorate the murder of the child by the signifier. Is this not one of the possible readings of Serge Leclaire's (1975) essay *On tue un enfant.*

A comparison can be made with what happens in the wooden-reel game. The appropriation of the symbolic game permits the child to master separation with the object and underlies the capacity to re-find it; but it can topple over into an excessive, narcissistic autarchy if it is premature.

Notes

1. Revised version of an intervention at the SPP (Paris Psychoanalytic Society) colloquium in Deauville in 1975, published in the *Revue française de psychanalyse*, 39(4), 1976.
2. See P. Aulagnier, *The Violence of Interpretation*, London: Routledge, 2001; and A. Green, *The Fabric of Affect in the Psychoanalytic Discourse*, London: Routledge, 1999.
3. See also the Conference on his book published in the *Revue française de psychanalyse*, XL, n° 4, 1976, pp. 733–740.

References

Freud, S. (1937). *Constructions in Analysis*. SE, 23.

Irigaray, L. (1966). 'Communication linguistique et spéculaire'. In *Cahiers d'analyse*, 3, Mai-Juin 1966, pp. 39–55.

Leclaire, S. (1975). *On tue un enfant. Un essai sur le narcissisme primaire et la pulsion de mort*. Paris : Le Seuil. [English version: *A Child is Being Killed: On Primary narcissism and the Death Drive*. Transl. M-C hays, Standford University Press, 1998]

Viderman, S. (1971). *La construction de l'espace analytique*. Paris: Denoël.

GENERAL BIBLIOGRAPHY

Aisenstein, M. (2001). 'Psychoanalytic psychotherapy does not exist'. In *Psychoanalysis and Psychotherapy: the Controversies and the Future* (chapter 2). London: Karnac Books.

Ameisen, J.C. (1999). *La sculpture du vivant: le suicide cellulaire ou la mort vivant*. Paris: Seuil.

Baldacci, J.L. (2005). 'Dès le début ... la sublimation?'. In *Revue française de Psychanalyse*, 2005/5, 1405–1474.

Bokanowski, T. (2004). 'Souffrance, destructivité, processus'. Report to the 64th Congress of French-speaking psychoanalysts in Milan, 2004. In *Revue française de psychanalyse*, 68(5).

Cahn, R. (2002). *La fin du divan*. Paris: Odile Jacob.

Conrad, J. (1900). *Lord Jim* (edited by Cedric Watts and Robert Hampson). London: Penguin, 1986.

Dispaux, M.-F. (2002). 'Aux sources de l'interprétation'. In *'L'agir et les processus de transformations'*, *Revue française de psychanalyse*, 66(5).

Donnet, J.-L. (1989). 'Symbolisation et règle fondamentale, le faire sens'. In *Revue française de Psychanalyse*, reporter A. Gibeault, vol. 53, 6.

Donnet, J.-L. (1995). *Le divan bien-tempéré*. Paris: Presses Universitaires de France.

Donnet, J.-L. (1995). *Le Divan bien tempéré*. [The well-tempered couch] Paris: Presses Universitaires de France, 'Le Fil rouge'.

Donnet, J.-L. (1997). 'L'Humoriste et sa croyance'. *Revue Française de Psychanalyse*, 61(3): 897–917.

Donnet, J.-L. (2005). 'Le Surmoi et les transformations du complexe d'Oedipe', *Libres Cahiers*, 12, Autumn 2005.

Donnet, J.-L. (2008). 'Le père et l'impersonnalisation du Surmoi. In *Hommage à André Green. Figures modernes du père*. Paris: Presses Universitaires de France.

Freud, S. (1900). *The Interpretation of Dreams. SE*, 4–5: 1–621

Freud, S. (1901). *The Psychopathology of Everyday Life. SE, 6*.

Freud, S. (1905a). *Jokes and their Relation to the Unconscious. SE, 8*.

Freud, S. (1905b). *Three Essays on the Theory of Sexuality. SE, 7*: 123–243.

Freud, S. (1910). *Leonard da Vinci and a Memory of his Childhood. SE, 11*: 57–137.

Freud, S. (1912). *The Dynamics of Transference. SE, 12*: 99–108.

Freud, S. (1912–1913). *Totem and Taboo. SE, 13*: 1–161.

Freud, S. (1913). *On Beginning the Treatment. SE, 12*.

Freud, S. (1914). *Remembering, Repeating and Working-Through. SE, 12*: 147–156.

Freud, S. (1919) '"A Child IS Being Beaten"', *SE, 17*: 177–204.

Freud, S. (1920). *Beyond the Pleasure Principle. SE* 18: 1–64.

Freud, S. (1921). *Group Psychology and the Analysis of the Ego. SE, 18*: 65–143.

Freud, S. (1923 [1922]). *Two Encaeclopaedia Articles. SE, 18*: 235–259.

Freud, S. (1924). *The Economic Problem of Masochism. SE, 19*: 155–170.

Freud, S. (1925). *Negation. SE, 19*: 233–239.

Freud, S. (1926). *The Question of Lay Analysis. SE, 20*: 183–258.

Freud, S. (1927). *Humour. SE, 21*: 160–166.

Freud, S. (1927). *The Future of an Illusion. SE, 21*: 1–56.

Freud, S. (1928). *Dostoevsky and Parricide. SE, 21*: 177–196.

Freud, S. (1930). *Civilization and its Discontents. SE, 21*: 59–145.

Freud, S. (1937). *Analysis Terminable and Interminable. SE, 23*: 209–253.

Freud, S. (1937). *Constructions in Analysis. SE, 23*: 255–269.

Freud, S. (1940 [1938]). *The Splitting of the Ego in the Process of Defence. SE, 23*: 271–278.

Freud, S. & Ferenczi, S. (2000). *The Correspondence of Sigmund Freud and Sandor Ferenczi*, vol. 3 (1923–1933), trans. P. Hoffer. Cambridge (Mass.): Harvard University Press.

Green, A. (1999). *The Work of the Negative*, trans. A. Weller. London: Free Association Books. [Originally published as *Le travail du negatif*, Paris: Editions de Minuit, 1993].

Green, A. (2002). *Psychoanalysis: a Paradigm for Clinical Thinking*, trans. A. Weller. London: Free Association Books.

Irigaray, L. (1966). 'Communication linguistique et spéculaire'. In *Cahiers d'analyse*, 3: Mai-Juin, 1966, pp. 39–55.

Israel, P. (1999). 'La psychanalyse et la psychothérapie analytique', *letter of the IPA*, 8(1): 14–18.

Leclaire, S. (1975). *On tue un enfant. Un essai sur le narcissisme primaire et la pulsion de mort*. Paris: Le Seuil. [English version: *A Child is Being Killed: On Primary narcissism and the Death Drive*. Transl. M-C hays, Standford University Press, 1998]

Le Guen, C.l. (1989). *Theorie de la méthode psychanalytique*, Paris, Presses Universitaires de France, «Le Fil rouge».

McDougall (1982). *Théatre du Je*. Paris: Gallimard.

Parat, C. (1998). *Affect partagé*. Paris: Presses Universitaires de France.

Parsons, M. (1999). 'The Logic of Play in Psychoanalysis'. *Int. J. Psychoanal.*, 80: 871–884.

Pasche, F. (1969). *A partir de Freud*. Paris: Payot.

Rolland, J.C. (2006). *Avant d être celui qui parle*. Paris: Gallimard.

Rosenberg, B. (1991). 'Le masochisme mortifère et masochisme gardien de la vie'. In *Le Masochisme*, Monograph, *Revue Psychanalyse Française*, Presses Universitaires de France.

Roussillon, R. (1995). 'La métapsychologie des processus et la transition-nalité'. Report to the 55th Congress of French-speaking psychoanalysts in 1995. In *Revue française de psychanalyse*, 59: Special Congress Issue, pp. 1351–1519.

Roussillon, R. (2004). 'Le jeu et le potentiel'. In *Revue française de Psychanalyse*, 68(1): 79–94.

Sechaud, E. (2005) 'Perdre, sublimer'. In *Revue française de Psychanalyse*, 2005/5.

Todorov, T. (1977). *Théories du symbole*. Paris: Le Seuil.

Todorov, T. (1978). *Symbolisme et interprétation*. Paris: Le Seuil.

Viderman, S. (1971). *La Construction de l'espace psychanalytique*. Paris: Denoël.

Wainrib, S. (2004). 'Là où çà joue', *Revue française de Psychanalyse*, 68(1).

Winnicott, D. (1968). 'Playing: Its theoretical status in the clinical situation' 1968, *Int J Psychoanal.*, 49.

Winnicott, D. (1971). *Playing and Reality*. London: Tavistock.

Zaltzman, N. (1998). *De la guérison psychanalytique*. Paris: Presses Universitaires de France

Zaltzmann, N. (2000). *De la guérison psychanalytique*. Paris: Presses Universitaires de France, 'Épîtres'.

INDEX

Defense mechanism 162
De-idealization 147
Depersonalisation 181
Derealization-depersonalization
  pairing 162
Desexualization and sexualization
  150
Desexualization characteristic
  121, 139
Desexualizing internalization 146
Diachronized organization
  of the transferential regression
  10, 91
Disorganizations-reorganizations 36
The Dynamics of Transference 28

The Economic Problem of
  Masochism 140
Ego
  dreamer 129
  humorist 151
  model 158
  task 121
  tiny 139
Egoism 111
Ego Psychology 44
Ego-Superego
  conflict 174
  differentiation 160
  introjection 175
  split 157
  system 32
Ego-Superego relations 140–141
  instinctual mitigation in 139
Embarkation 127
Encounter and consultation 83–87
Epistemological rupture 43
Epistemological status 2
  theorization 2

Face-to-face situation 73, 77
Fading 46

Fain, Michel 59
Feminine passivation 127
Ferenczi's abrupt formula 69
Free-floating listening 10
French
  gunboat 94
  psychoanalytic culture 4
  sailing terminology 87
  semantic context 91
Freud
  allusion 146
  analysis of the fantasy 17
  aphorism 160
  attachment 23
  Civilization and its Discontents
    76
  conviction 59
  difficulties 92, 155
  floating listening 46
  formulation 144
  inaugural invention 42
  indications 168
  metaphor on transference-
    love 31
  mind 161
  nonetheless 9
  position 141, 170
  preference for a method
    operating 22
  psychoanalytic procedure 57
  reservations 138
  text and difficulties 155
Freudian
  agieren ('enactment') 91
  concept 153
  conception of the
    significance 113
  discovery 43
  humour 162
  idea of a work of culture 13
  inconsistencies 92
  invention 22

CPSIA information can be obtained
at www.ICGtesting.com
Printed in the USA
LVHW020826240523
747800LV00017B/1279